Helping Ghosts

Helping Ghosts

A Guide to Understanding Lost Spirits

by Louis Charles

"An idea, like a ghost, must be spoken to a little before it will explain itself." - Charles Dickens

Helping Ghosts: A Guide to Understanding Lost Spirits
Copyright 2010 by Louis Charles   All rights reserved.

No part of this publication may be reproduced, storied in a retrievable system, or transmitted in any way by any means, electronic, mechanical, photocopy, recording, or otherwise without prior written permission of the author except as provided by USA copyright law.
Translations of biblical texts are from the King James Version Bible or from the author.
Other quotations cited within this book are used with permission unless generally considered to be in the public domain.

Published by Angels & Ghosts, LLC dba Angels & Ghosts Publishing
c/o AngelsGhosts.com and Author Louis Charles
lcdupla@yahoo.com
Cover design and artwork by Angels & Ghosts Publishing
Copyright 2010 Angels & Ghosts, LLC

Published in the United States of America
ISBN: 145284707X
EAN-13: 9781452847078
Non-Fiction: Body, Mind & Spirit/ Supernatural
1. Ghosts 2. Spirits

Helping Ghosts is dedicated to my grandmother, Audrey.

We never had the chance to meet face to face, but you still make your presence known.

Acknowledgements

My experiences that led to writing *Helping Ghosts* have been a journey that I shared with many others.

I want to first thank my family for their understanding and love. Without them, this book would not have been possible. Thank you, Becky, Trey, Chad, and Amelia.

I also wish to give thanks to many special people who have assisted me, given me inspiration, or shared their personal experiences. Without them, the insights I share in *Helping Ghosts* would not have been possible. Thank you *SIGHT* team, especially Laura Lyn and Christopher Reed. My sincere appreciation also goes to Hans Holzer, Frank Sumption, Dr. Edith Fiore, Kathy Owen, Polly Gear, Sherri Brake, Rob Schwartz, Mike Cistone, Steve Hultay, Bruce Halliday, Dale Lute, Ben Hockenberry, Martin Jackson, and Walt Bissell.

Contents

Forward

The writing of *Helping Ghosts* has afforded me the time to look back on my life and the experiences I have had with ghosts. What you are about to read is my honest attempt toward understanding what can happen after death of the body if the soul of the person is unable to transition from this world easily.

After seeing a predominance of fearful teachings about ghosts on television and the Internet, I decided to share my experiments, findings, and practices by book. There is much misunderstanding about ghosts and their behavior. I hope to encourage and educate both people who suffer a haunting and those who investigate and desire to solve ghost problems.

Within Western society, religion is the basis of many commonly-held beliefs, creating fears about ghosts and death. In order to address the source of these fears properly, I found it necessary to quote some biblical texts that shed light upon helping ghosts throughout this book. Although I share such passages, my insights and methods for ghost rescue are non-religious. Because some of the concepts I convey may be new to the reader, I attempted to be somewhat repetitive as I reveal core ideas through my personal experiences, then later, through more detailed explanation. My goal has been to encourage the reader to help ghosts, too. After reading the book, I trust you will understand how to help ghosts, complete with methods you will find useful.

Throughout my journey, I have had unseen helpers along the way. I remain thankful for the insights I have received from them. Even as I worked on the final touches of the manuscript for *Helping Ghosts*, the experiences and experiments continued...

Chapter One

Spirits in the Material

I often reflect back to when I was a young boy living out in the Ohio countryside. Nature was my playground, and playmates were few and far between. I frequently played alone in the yard, field, or in our fruit trees. I loved eating green apples and collecting tent worms from among the tree branches. Life was much simpler then, and I was eager to explore and learn about the world around me.

One memory, that I fondly recall, takes me back almost forty years to a warm summer day when I was maybe six or seven years old. It was early afternoon. I was sitting beneath our tall elm trees enjoying a bright orange Popsicle. Goldfinches, or even a blackbird or two, noisily gathered in the canopy high above me. Surrounded by lilac bushes, trees, and rock gardens, my eyes longed to take in more of nature's beauty while I enjoyed my cool treat. As a boy, I loved nature and longed to be outdoors as much as possible.

When I finished eating, I just happened to look upward to catch sight of a beautiful monarch butterfly floating slightly above me. I had seen butterflies before, but something was strangely different with this one. This graceful insect happily toyed with me. It danced up and down on the air like a yo-yo on a string. When I waved my empty Popsicle stick in the sky like a swordsman, the butterfly swooped back and forth in sync, enjoying every "swoosh" of our little game! As our contest went on for awhile, I could hardly believe how much fun it was to have this seemingly insignificant insect play with me. I enjoyed watching him dodge every swing of my "sword." This insect became my instant friend, and friends were not something to be wasted.

Having become a bit too eager to win the game, I accidentally struck the butterfly. My wooden stick ripped through its fragile, paper like wing in the middle of our fun. To my horror, he plummeted to the ground being reduced to a fallen, twitching creature at my feet. I could easily see one of his wings had been torn in two, and I knew the insect's days of flight were now over. Tears flowed down my cheeks as I felt heartbreak and desperation.

I knew in my mind that somehow I had to make this right. I decided to scoop up the black and orange butterfly, gently placing him in my red plastic fireman's helmet found in our garage. With tear-streamed cheeks, I showed my mom the helmet and my little friend inside of it.

"What can I do?" I sobbed.

"Take the butterfly into our garden and ask God for His help," she replied.

We hardly ever went to church, but my parents still had a belief in a higher power. The idea of praying to God for help was something foreign to me at the time, but I was desperate and willing to attempt anything to save the little butterfly.

Our garden was a good walk behind our two-story house, and all sorts of weeds had taken over that season. While I struggled to push my way through the tall vegetation, I decided not to enter very deep. In a strange way, the plants sort of surrounded me and the butterfly like walls of a sanctuary. Kneeling down with the injured creature still in my helmet, I placed it in front of me. I began crying out to God. To this day, I still don't recall what I said. Perhaps, it wasn't even what I said that was important. I just remember the childlike faith of a little boy who trusted with his whole heart the direction of his parents. While at a young age, I was completely incapable of doubting anything my mother told me. If she said it was so, to me, it had to be true.

"The butterfly must be healed," I thought to myself wholeheartedly.

I cried out my petition until there was nothing left to plea. Then, my swollen, soaked eyes glanced up to see it happen. The monarch butterfly slowly and deliberately walked up onto the brim of the helmet, stretched forth his perfect wings, and looked me in the eye for maybe twenty seconds. I don't know how I knew it, but I am certain to this day that the insect waited until it was sure I would observe the miracle. In a moment of triumph, he took flight, never to be seen by me again. Perhaps the release of guilt I felt inside meant the most to me that day. I was freed knowing I had not destroyed the beautiful butterfly. Now, as my thoughts retrace the event, I can't help but wonder where that little boy went. For a moment in time, I had been a child who did not doubt but knew the power of the unseen to make a fallen thing right. Like the monarch butterfly, that little boy also disappeared.

I often recount that story to others when I share my spiritual journey. The miracle of the monarch butterfly is an example of how children often have fantastic experiences with spirit, more so than most adults. Over time, the awareness of the unseen seems to dissipate as our minds become more and more conditioned to the external world around us. Then, it becomes difficult to believe that anything could exist beyond the range of the physical environment and our five senses. For me, it was no different.

When I was young, I remember loving the color green. My mother, however, loved blue. Her passion for the color blue was so strong that she eventually and unintentionally convinced me that my love for green was invalid.

"You like green? What about blue?" I recall her questioning me.

Because I highly valued the opinion of my parents, I soon found myself disliking green. I can remember telling my teachers and friends at school that my favorite color was blue. It wasn't until about ten years ago that I realized blue is not my favorite color. Don't get me wrong. I like blue, but today my wife will tell you my closet and drawers are filled with green clothing. Although I thought I had personally chosen blue as my favorite color, I subconsciously preferred a different hue. I love green. This small example has caused me to wonder about our childhood experiences. How much of what we believe about ourselves is actually true? Could some of our beliefs be a product of conditioning?

As a youth, I also remember being captivated by the idea of

ghosts and haunting. My hidden, childhood fascination with spirits would later surface and become important to me as an adult. Looking back upon my life today, I can recall many seeds being planted within me about ghosts. For example, Halloween was my favorite holiday. I thoroughly enjoyed dressing up as monsters. A visit to *Universal Studios* further fueled my intrigue of the paranormal. I convinced my parents to buy me a Frankenstein mask while at the theme park. When we visited *Disneyland* days later, my parents allowed me to ride the *Haunted Mansion* attraction. Both of these experiences inspired me to make horror props while still in grade school. Although I didn't understand why I was intrigued, my interest in ghosts still ran deep.

You probably guessed by now that *Scooby-Doo* was my favorite cartoon to watch on Saturday mornings. While investigating spooky legends and solving crimes, Scooby and the gang would occasionally encounter a real ghost. I always became glued to television shows that featured haunting. Even re-runs of *Three Stooges* shorts had the bumbling trio encountering a real specter from time to time! The possibility of unseen people walking the earth became fascinating to me. TV, movies, and books piqued my curiosity about the unexplained throughout my childhood.

When the movie *Ghost Busters* became all the rage in the 1980s, I was a young adult. I watched the film and wished I could also detect and capture ghosts. Hollywood, specifically movies, cartoons, and television programs, had eventually taught me that ghosts existed but were bad. Who wouldn't want to save the living from the dead? After all, ghosts were something most people feared; they had to be bad, right? Today, many of the reality TV ghost hunting shows are still reinforcing this age-old belief.

Like many, my cultural experiences had generally taught me that ghosts were something to fear. I had learned there couldn't be such a thing as a good ghost, though *Casper the Friendly Ghost* might disagree. This belief of mine only intensified after I became a Fundamentalist Christian as a young adult. Oftentimes, Christianity teaches that when a person dies, he or she is either blissfully living in Heaven or suffering for all of eternity in a fiery Hell. Consequently, Christian denominations typically do not subscribe to the existence of ghosts. This is because most Christian teachings do not allow for any other place or state of the dead. The idea that a human spirit could walk among the living is often taught to be impossible. If someone claims to have seen a ghost, it is usually equated with being a demon. Believers are taught that Satan is out to deceive all of humanity; therefore, ghosts are thought to be devils in disguise wreaking havoc on the unwise.

It's safe to say that for the next ten years of my life, the idea that ghosts might exist became quite difficult for me to even consider. I had closed my mind to the idea. Eventually, my interest in ghosts abated even though deep down I was subtly nagged by my suppressed thoughts about them. Having fully succumbed to my religious fear, I had become a staunch, Bible-bound Christian; and the "good book" was what I had elected to follow instead of my heart.

In my prior book, *Jesus Religion*, I shared how I eventually had a spiritual awakening that changed my legalistic perspective. For the first time in my life, I became aware of a tangible spirit presence. Having been devoutly religious for about a decade at this point in my life, I had not been aware that spirit energy could be experienced, felt. Imagine the shock as my world was turned upside down! I felt as though someone suddenly turned lights on that revealed a new direction for my life.

My awakening to spirit did not happen at church but at home one day. The strong presence stayed with me for about a week, and I felt an intense love, peace, and joy associated with it. More importantly, I also awoke to a voice submerged within my heart that accompanied the tangible, spirit presence. I can only equate this voice with being a "knowing inside me." As I quieted the thoughts of my mind, I could hear the voice much better; therefore, meditation became my path toward recognizing what emanated from within my deepest being.

At that time, I initially equated this voice with being direct communication from God. I suppose I did so because I was staunchly religious. I had the habit of interpreting everything in my life as either a blessing from God or an attack from the Devil. So to me, my interpretation of the voice was that it was good; and good must be God. The voice's presence caused me to feel peace, love, and joy like I had never felt before in my life. Could such a spirit be anything but good? The voice also shared truths that helped me to become free from various forms of fear.

By continually striving to listen to the words deep inside me, eventually I no longer believed in separation, eternal punishment, demons, Satan, or an angry god for that matter. To me, there was only good. We are all a part of it, and it was God.

After several years of following the voice within, one might say I had an epiphany one day. I distinctly remember meditating and listening to what was within my heart. To my surprise, it was revealed to me that messengers, people in spirit, had been speaking to me as well. This tangible, spirit presence, I had come to love, had benevolent spirits contained within it who were enlightened and sharing ideas with me!

Suddenly, more of my experiences began to make sense to me. I could recall occasionally being caressed or feeling someone breathe on the back of my neck during these enlightened communications. I felt love being expressed to me by others in spirit. How grand that was! I realized the energy that animates everything was not only in me and other people, but everyone and everything is within this higher power. A mystery, for me, had been solved. My newly found oneness with the universe was a grand secret that I had not been able to embrace before my awakening.

My mind was numb with the ideas that were filling it, and I could only wonder about my former, religious beliefs of people being eternally lost, separated from each other due to their sins. I no longer could believe in a fiery place of punishment. The fear of Hell was dead in me. Still, I wondered what happens to those who are full of hatred, anger, condemnation, worthlessness and other forms of suffering. Where do they go after their bodies expire? Wouldn't they also be a part of this peaceful spirit energy I experienced? If so, how could they remain in a state of torment? I wanted answers. If people did continue to suffer, how could that be possible? Where would they suffer? The questions kept filling my head.

I began searching my heart concerning the fate of humanity after my spiritual awakening. This is when I began visualizing what I suspected could be occurring with a part of mankind. When a body dies, I realized the person could remain temporarily lost, especially if they were not aware of their higher self. I theorized that hurting people might unwittingly choose to stay on a path of suffering. Becoming lost was not a condition produced from having an informed choice, and it was not a judgment emanating from a condemning god. It was like being adrift at sea, unaware of where to go or how to navigate home. Someone needed to be a beacon and shine light in order to bring the abandoned to shore, to aid the lost from their disorientation. We often see people around us who need guidance. Why wouldn't disembodied human souls possibly need guidance, too? I realized that the state of not knowing who we truly are is hell. People do not have to die in order to experience hell, for hell is not a place of suffering but a state of mind. If some people are pained by emotional trauma today, are we to believe that the death of their body will instantly heal their mind?

I soon found myself attempting to correlate my thoughts about lost spirits with biblical passages that came to remembrance. Could ghosts be found in the Bible? In I Samuel

28:15, King Saul visits a medium and asks her to bring forth Samuel from the grave so he may speak with the dead prophet.

"And Samuel said to Saul, 'Why did you trouble me to bring me up?'"

Whether a ghost or spirit, Samuel was somehow able to speak with the living even though his body had expired. This story conveys that the dead are among us and able to communicate. I also found it interesting to read that the spirit of Samuel is described wearing the same clothes he wore in his earthly life. Was this time-honored prophet still living in the past?

As I further considered scriptures, I recalled in Mark 9:4 that Moses and Elijah allegedly appeared to Jesus and spoke with him.

"...and there appeared to them Elijah and Moses, and they were talking with Jesus."

The bodies of Moses and Elijah had perished well before the time of Jesus. Yet, they appeared and chatted with Jesus? This passage also affirms the idea that human spirits can communicate with us from the other side of the grave. It's even more interesting to consider that we read Jesus chose to reveal this to a select few: Peter, James, and John. It, therefore, must have been an important truth for them to understand.

The idea that disembodied human spirits interact with us can be found elsewhere in the Bible. A well known passage in Hebrews Chapter 12 indicates that human souls are not in another place but remain among the living.

"...we also have a great cloud of witnesses set around us."

These are not the only examples of spirits found within the Bible. After the crucifixion of Jesus, it is reported that he appeared in spirit form to different people. Stories of him manifesting in the midst of followers is very similar to modern-day ghost sightings. We read that after his death, other ghosts or spirits were seen, too.

"*...and the tombs were opened, and many bodies of the saints who have fallen asleep, arose; and having come forth out of the tombs after Jesus' rising, they went into the holy city and appeared to many.*" - Matthew 27:52-53

If this scene is not ghostly enough for you to imagine, do you recall the story of Jesus walking upon the water to meet his disciples? I must point out that the word *phantasma* (meaning apparition, a ghost) is used in the text's original language.

"*...and the disciples having seen him walking upon the sea were troubled saying, 'It is an apparition.' and from the fear they cried out.*" - Matthew 14:26

The men thought they were seeing a ghost. It is obvious from this passage, and the others I have shared, that people during the time of Jesus held strong beliefs about ghosts and spirits. How could some Christian denominations choose to deny their existence? Bible verses eventually convinced me that what I had originally learned about ghosts, while a Christian, was not true.

In December of 2002, I launched the website *Jesus Religion* in order to share some of these ideas I had been hearing within me. My goal was to help others who were struggling with some of the same fearful teachings I had once believed. Soon, I found myself also creating a web page devoted to ghosts in the Bible. By 2004, I had an even deeper desire to study ghosts and spirits further. I wanted to approach my research of the paranormal a bit differently. An idea had been birthed in me to gather and study evidence of spirits from around the world for comparison. I wanted to collect stories, photographs, videos, and audio evidence of spirits through use of the Internet. It was then that I created a new website for my project. I called it *Angels & Ghosts*. Not only would I collect and share the evidence, but I would allow the visitors of my website to come to their own conclusions about the information. I wasn't concerned with being able to validate all of the submissions. I simply wanted to provide a resource for those who also wished to study potential evidence of ghosts and spirits. Yes, people needed to make up their own minds about the paranormal. After all, life is a journey made up of personal experiences.

As the *Angels & Ghosts* website grew in size, I began realizing I needed to incorporate my spiritual ideas into its pages. I noticed a void within the paranormal TV shows that were rising in popularity. Ghosts were not being studied to understand their condition. Television producers were more interested in promoting fear than reason to gain viewers. At times, supposed evidence of ghosts seemed manufactured, all for the sake of ratings. Ghosts were not viewed as human spirits in need of compassion but rather as unseen vapors from the unknown; they were something to fear, even taunt while attempting to prove to the TV audience they existed. Personally, I did not need proof that the spirits of people survive after death, and I wasn't interested in fearful interpretations of the paranormal. I wanted to understand why ghosts existed and how I could help. Most importantly, to me, ghosts were (and are) hurting people.

I no longer was able to view the world as being separate from myself. In my mind, this included everyone and everything. I knew in my heart that people, whether on this side of the grave or beyond, are one-energy, one spirit. If humanity is collectively animated by a single, greater energy, then I concluded we can never truly be separate from each other, even though thoughts of division might seem plausible.

For many of us, death has become the symbol of separation. We believe it divides us from people who rest in graves. Due to the voice of higher consciousness which rose up within me, I began to consider death differently. I wondered if death were only an illusion, something we fear only because we believe it has disconnected us from others in the ethereal realms. Would death relinquish its power over the mind if we knew loved ones were with us in spirit? I needed to find out if the disembodied walk among us, ever attempting to communicate with people of the earth. If I found this to be so, would I be willing to share their story with the world in order to bring light to the forgotten? I was about to find the answers to these questions and more.

Chapter Two

There is No Other Side

As I studied ghosts through books, television, websites, and the evidence I was collecting from around the world via my website, I was fascinated at what I was learning. There were many theories regarding ghosts and haunting. To me, many of the ideas concerning the paranormal seemed to be based more upon fear and fable. Throughout my studies, the voice that reasoned deep within me kept me away from believing in fearful ideas, always revealing a non-threatening understanding of the unknown. I was continually compelled to look beyond the fear toward rational and more logical explanations.

When I think of the word "ghost," it doesn't sound so friendly, often bringing to mind eerie representations of monstrous beings from the nether world. A ghost, by my definition, is simply a label for a disembodied human or animal spirit. All of us are spirit, a word I use interchangeably with the word "energy." A spirit is comprised of intelligence, being a part of a vast conscious energy that animates all life. Everything, including all of humanity, exists within this intelligent energy and is connected.

Although the ghosts I am writing about are intelligent, there is phenomena that some ghost investigators consider to be unintelligent. Poltergeists, or *noisy ghosts*, have often been theorized to be a form of psychokinesis. In a poltergeist-type of haunting, it is common for inanimate objects to move, electrical appliances to turn on by themselves, or strange sounds to be heard such as knocking on walls. Because poltergeist-type activity often occurs in homes where a teenager resides (usually female), some parapsychologists have speculated that the manipulation of objects by an invisible force could be accidentally caused by the child. They suspect that the emotional, teenage mind might remain unaware of its short-lived ability to move inanimate items. Other researchers, however, have suggested that perhaps poltergeist activity is not unintelligent but the result of ghosts who become active by using the energy of those in the household. They speculate the entity is able to find empowerment through an emotional teenager or negative adult, enhancing the ghost's ability to interact with people.

In another example of unintelligent haunting, human apparitions have been witnessed that are completely unaware of the physical environment. They may walk through walls, be oblivious to people around them, or continue the exact same activity as when viewed before. Some believe this type of spirit to be residual energy left over from a prior life. It is theorized that such ghosts are simply glimpses of the past that somehow replay over and over, an unexplainable loop in time, much like watching an old movie unfold on the television screen. Other spirit energies are believed to be clouds of negativity imprinted on the environment, created during some sort of traumatic episode. It is thought that these negative fields can still have influence and detrimental effects on the living. All of these examples that I have described are commonly believed to be unintelligent types of haunting. They are not believed to be real ghosts. Paranormal investigators typically rationalize them as aimless occurrences within the human experience. Even though such theories are intriguing, I have wondered if ghost investigators have been too quick to categorize paranormal experiences into types of haunting, myself included. We just might find that some of these abnormal encounters could simply be variations in ghost personality, purpose and suffering, something that occasionally manifests that we do not fully understand. Although this might not explain every strange encounter we may have with the unknown, it should at least cause us to reconsider ghosts and their behavior.

The belief that the human spirit survives death of the physical body is found within most religions, but not every faith teaches the existence of ghosts or how to help them. It is interesting that Judaism, Buddhism, and Hinduism have teachings about ghosts; that they are suffering human spirits. Interestingly, it is taught by certain sects within these religions that suffering souls often need our help to move beyond their emotional trauma. Yet within Western society, our culture has not readily embraced the idea of ghosts being impaired, human spirits whom we can help. We seem unaware of this idea. It would appear we prefer to view ghosts from a frightening perspective, or we simply do not want to know they exist at all.

As I continued on a quest to see beyond conventional ideas concerning ghosts, the *Angels & Ghosts* website grew in size. E-mails of submissions eventually provided me with more and more ghost photographs to compare. After looking at thousands of potential ghost pictures, I eventually suspected that many of the photos did not contain images of ghosts at all. I contacted a paranormal investigator and friend of mine, Kathy Owen, and asked if she would help conduct several experiments using digital cameras. Kathy kindly obliged and photographed all sorts of things for me, such as cigarette smoke, human breath in cold air, snow, rain, dust, and reflective surfaces. She also took photographs utilizing various camera settings, different exposure times, and with her finger placed over the flash unit to see what would happen. We soon knew for certain that quite a bit of the anomalies we see in photographs could be explained by accidental misuse of the camera or natural explanations.

Compact, digital cameras with lots of features have inadvertently created a wave of purportedly paranormal photographs. Flash units situated close to the camera's lens will often produce false balls of light that look like orbs. These smaller cameras also make it too easy for a stray finger from the photographer to partially cover the flash unit. This can occasionally produce strange shadows in photographs. Special camera modes that lengthen the exposure seem to also play a role in many of the anomalies. One camera mode, in particular, is sometimes referred to as "night time" flash setting. False apparitions, light bars, orange haze, and blurry photographs are typically produced by this setting that is only to be used with a tripod. Although many people use this feature at night during ghost investigation, some remain unaware that the slightest movement of the camera will cause these effects in their photos.

Kathy and I also found that many natural occurrences, such as moisture from rain, snow, fog, or even a nearby fountain can produce balls of light within photographs due to the camera's flash reflecting off of minuscule, airborne water droplets. In fact, most orbs that people believe to be ghosts are actually caused by the flash reflecting off of dust or pollen particles floating near the lens of the camera. We can even be fooled by smudges on the lens or by warm, human breath in a cold environment, both creating very believable mists that may appear to be spirits posing for a picture!

When we cannot find a normal explanation for some of the anomalies found within ghost pictures, we must conclude they are possibly paranormal in nature. Still, even these captures of ghosts and spirits differ at times. A spirit might be recorded by the camera as a ball of light called an orb, or perhaps as a misty vapor, a dark shadow, or a see-through person called an apparition. Orbs, strange streaks of light, white mists, and vaporous apparitions all appear to be manifestations of a higher energy frequency, that being light. This is quite opposite of the shadowy images of ghosts. It intrigued me that ghost manifestations found within photographs varied from light to dark, from a *pure* energy to what I'll deem as appearing to be "unclean." I couldn't help but wonder what the significance of this meant.

In some ghost photographs, the spirit of a human being will be seen and captured as a moving shadow. This type of ghost is known as a "shadow ghost, "shade," or "dark shadow." When I began studying the dark, human forms, I wondered if the shadowed appearance meant the ghost was of a different type or if the darkness that filled the ghost had significance. Many of us have learned to equate darkness with being something bad. Consequently, a ghost observed as a moving shadow is typically misunderstood and feared. I chose not to jump to conclusions, allowing myself to meditate upon a question: Why does the appearance of some ghosts look dark? As I thought about this further, I eventually came to understand that the darkness represented the mental and emotional state of the disembodied person. The different degrees of light or darkness that a ghost might manifest reveal their inner condition. A dark countenance of a spirit is the visible sign that the person is lost, meaning unenlightened.

Around this time, I became aware of Polly Gear, a lady who had captured one of the best images of a shadow ghost that I had seen. The photograph was taken inside the *West Virginia State Penitentiary* located in Moundsville, West Virginia, near the Ohio River. I contacted Polly and asked if I could visit the abandoned prison with her in order to hear her account firsthand. She politely obliged. I really was inspired to write an article about her amazing photo as well as learn more about shadow ghosts that might aid my developing theory.

Polly agreed to retell the incident to me in-person at the prison. As we neared the end of the long hallway where the ghost had been recorded by her camera, she began sharing with me her surprising story about what she had experienced. Prior to Polly's encounter with the shadow ghost, she had been coming to the prison for about five years to do ghost investigation. She had never previously seen a shadow ghost at the old penitentiary prior to that night in 2004. After a severe thunder and lightning storm, she heard a noise behind her near the doorway that led toward the cafeteria. With flashlight in hand, she proceeded from the hallway to the doorway leading to a small corridor that connects to the cafeteria. Polly wanted to see if she could determine what could have made the sound. When she reached the doorway, she turned on her flashlight and spotted a black, human form walking from the cafeteria toward her in the small corridor. The shadowy figure was that of a man apparently looking out the windows to his right as he walked. Polly's flashlight shined through the dark ghost, whom she described as looking similar to "black static appearing on a TV." The ghost noticed the light penetrating his arm, looked at Polly, and then made a quick dash toward the door frame to hide in the darkness of the corner. While the shadow man moved toward the door frame to hide, Polly moved backward out of his way and up the big hallway from where she had come, turning her camera on in the process. She instinctively knew that if she did not leave the area of the doorway first, the ghost would likely leave the opposite direction. After waiting a few seconds for the camera to turn on, she aimed it into the dark and toward the doorway approximately 110 feet away. Unknown to her at the time, Polly Gear snapped an incredible photograph of the now famous *Moundsville Shadow Man*.

Polly Gear's photograph of the dark shadow reveals the perfect shape of a rather large man. During the time of her encounter, she could not detect any facial details, hair, or sounds emanating from the ghost. The specter moved as if it was animated. Being of intelligence, the shadow figure was quite aware of Polly and interacted with her presence. She told me she was not afraid of this ghost at all and felt that he was just as curious about her as she was of him. Polly does not believe the male spirit had any evil intentions. A few years later, a visitor to the *Angels & Ghosts* website sent me another photograph of a shadowed, ghost man. It was also taken from within the same kitchen area at the prison. It further corroborates Polly Gear's evidence and story of the shadow man at *Moundsville Penitentiary*.

There are some paranormal investigators who choose to believe that shadow ghosts must be either demons or negative human spirits. This interpretation does not necessarily correspond to findings by others who also study ghosts, especially those who have captured video or photographs of both adults and children in shadowed form. Polly Gear's shadow man story, along with other accounts I have collected, reveals that dark, moving shadows are often intelligent, interactive, and human in appearance. Their dark form does not always seem to be an indicator of ill-intentions but more often a visible expression of being lost or afraid. Just like the people we see every day in the physical world, ghosts may vary in size, shape and personality; therefore, it is not surprising to me that shadow-type entities have been observed occasionally having red eyes, or wearing a hood, or even donning a hat! Although they may have different personalities and intentions, shadow ghosts are more likely to be noticed during the evening; darkness possibly providing a better cloak from which to move in and out. At night time, they have been observed appearing beside people's beds, perhaps in an attempt to communicate with the unsuspecting who are asleep.

Photographs and stories of ghosts manifesting as dark entities caused me to think more about this state and how it relates to light. Darkness itself is simply a lack of light. Eventually, my higher consciousness brought my attention to a verse concerning light that is attributed to Jesus.

"You are the light of the world....let your light shine before men that they may see your good works." – excerpted from Matthew 5:14, 16

This intrigued me. I prefer to view biblical passages as allegories, meaning they convey figurative ideas, not messages to be understood literally. As I considered this verse, I wondered if it could be alluding that our true, inner condition can be seen by others, especially after the physical body has perished. I liked interpreting this verse in an allegorical manner, and it was another passage that convinced me further of this:

The eye is the lamp of the body. If your eyes are good, your whole body will be full of light. But if your eyes are bad, your whole body will be full of darkness. If then the light within you is darkness, how great is that darkness! - Matthew 6-22-23 (NIV)

Is the condition of our soul visible to others? In the above parable, it became obvious to me that the eye represents what our lives are focused upon. After all, it has been said that a man without vision will perish. I have observed that many people are living lives solely focused on what is taking place outside of them. We tend to base our existence upon the information our five senses, especially our eyes, gather and bring to the brain for interpretation. Convinced that this method of gathering data is the only source for truth, the five senses and brain become our god and guide through life. This lifestyle pattern unfortunately causes us to forget to search deep inside our being for direction and enlightenment. Being lost without vision, without direction, and without understanding, we then stumble about in darkness. The light is the knowledge and source of truth that resides deep within every soul, the real person hiding behind a wall of flesh and bones. This light of truth is incorruptible, ever present, and eternal. Although the light to guide us shines within our being, we can remain unaware; and therefore, unable to follow that light. This allows the darkness of misunderstanding to cloud our thinking. Through this idea of light and darkness, what is within is without; and what appears to be outside of us really emanates from inside. We create and experience from what we choose to follow, whether it is the light of truth or its seeming absence, darkness and misunderstanding.

As my mind tossed these ideas about, it became quite clear to me that there is a spiritual distinction to be made between light and dark, something that could be used to distinguish a difference between entities.

"What are the differences between ghosts and spirits?" I wondered. My mind continued to dwell upon this.

I previously shared that all of us are a part of a single energy that we may call, "spirit." I began to suppose that some expression of thought within the whole intelligence of spirit could originate from individual spirit entities. In other words, each person could be viewed as a group of thoughts existing within a vast, divine mind. Some of these thoughts within each group might be false, while others could be true. The thoughts themselves were also spirit energy. As we journey through life and learn, lower-energy thoughts would eventually dissipate until we are left with more truth than fiction in our thinking. What we choose to believe, we put our energy behind. As we come to know truth, the false dissipates and is no longer recognized. I suspect that the knowledge of truth is shared with everyone and everything within the single energy. We share our experiences and learning with one another through the common, interwoven thread of spirit. To awaken to the all-knowing spirit, we need only listen closely for the voice that is within each of us. This vision became my personal view of enlightenment. Still, I felt a distinction needed to be drawn between spirits who were enlightened to the light of truth within and those who would need awakened to this same understanding. Within my model, it would appear some spirits could be more enlightened than others. In example, a portion could be elevated in knowledge and closer to pure light, while others might be lost for awhile, existing within absolute darkness. Of course, there could be every conceivable variation of spirit condition found in-between.

"That" I surmised, "could be the difference between ghosts and spirits."

In my thinking, ghosts would not be second-class citizens when compared to spirits who dwell in light, even if they are temporarily mentally-disconnected from the truth that connects all humanity. I imagined that most ghosts did not knowingly ask to be in such a wretched condition. Maybe, knowing a simple truth could be the difference between the soul of a person suffering in darkness for a season or the person finding their freedom to move onward in the journey of life. This idea caused me to want to understand more about what caused a person to become a ghost in the first place.

When one thinks rationally, if ghosts are truly suffering people, would it make sense to just forget about disembodied humans if we should encounter them? I would find it difficult to do that. To some, the thought of a ghost walking among us might imply that such an entity is not a complete human being but only a remnant of the former person. To believe so appears to be a fore drawn conclusion perhaps created out of fear; therefore it is likely a misconception. We need to help each other. Within certain societies mankind has the tendency to sweep the crumbs under the table, so to speak. We may sadly choose to forget about our elderly, our poor, and our afflicted, especially if we want to believe they are somehow different and separate from us. After all, it's a bother to care for someone else other than ourselves. It's their problem, not ours, now isn't it? Should I expect we might think differently about something as incorporeal as ghosts?

"Ah, let God deal with them. It's his mess anyway, right?" people might conclude.

I think our complacency and lack of expressing love toward others has become epidemic at times, much like a virus that has sickened the hearts of many. This is the true plight of humanity in this new age. While considering human peril, I wondered what happens to us when we die. Can we make a difference in the lives of the unseen? If we make a difference, will it also change lives here on earth?

My curiosity compelled me to further investigate ghosts and their state of suffering through first studying near death experiences, NDEs for short. Knowing that NDEs vary from the good to the bad, I wanted to identify the common thread that was interwoven within most of them. What I found within the tapestry of the near death experience was very interesting to me. There are often three major events described by those who have died and have come back to tell us about it. Could these stories of what happens to us when the body dies shed light on the condition of ghosts? I believed so.

The first experience many report during the dying process of the body, when the soul of the person is freed, is being greeted by loved ones. It is common for one or more deceased family members, friends, or maybe an unknown, loving spirit to choose to assist the dying person with their transition from this world unto the next. Their loving communication is a guide and comfort to the spirit who is about to leave the past, earthly experience behind for good. We might consider these messengers to be benevolent angels of death. They help ease the mind of its fear so we can continue the life-journey beyond this physical plane. This greeting and communication from loving spirits is not only witnessed by people whose bodies are expiring but sometimes by the people who are in the room with them. Many who work in nursing care facilities or hospitals have shared stories of observing patients carry on conversations with unseen people before they die. At times, they might be fortunate enough to actually hear spirit voices or catch a glimpse of their vaporous visage. On occasion, some have even witnessed the spirit leave the body at the time of death. What a comfort to know we are spirits who are loved and cared for to such a degree!

I once heard someone say, "We are born into this world alone, and we must leave this world the same way," but I disagree. All of us come into this world from within the womb of a mother, hopefully being greeted by her and others. Our first earthly experience is not something we should share alone. Good parents comfort and protect their newly-born child, helping the infant adjust to the unfamiliar environment. Likewise, death is not something we will experience alone. If we are not alone at the birth of our body, why would we expect to be alone when the time has come for the body to expire? People who observe the dying process of another might not perceive that there are enlightened beings with them, but loving spirits are there just the same welcoming each and every soul to the light. Death and the unknown can be a fearful prospect for many; therefore, helpful spirits are with us while the body expires in order to bring love, comfort, and understanding to the fearing mind.

When I first learned of death bed visitors, I knew instantly that these loving guides have a greater purpose beyond just saying "hello" to those whose earthly lives have drawn to a close. They work to insure the dying move forward and toward the light, often accompanying them the entire way. In fact, seeing the presence of a great light is the second major event most people report from their near death experiences.

A "tunnel of light" is often encountered in the near death experience. It is not uncommon, however, for the light to appear in various forms. Some have described seeing a wall of light, a place of light, a ball of light, or even a light beam within different near death scenarios. There are no rules for how the light must appear to us; it would seem we will experience just what we need to see in order to seize the light that originates from within our higher consciousness.

People who have been embraced by this light will share that it is indescribable. The pureness of the light has been equated with the feeling of overwhelming, pure love. It is a revitalizing experience that brings unequaled peace and joy. During the near death experience, the person who has discovered this light wishes to remain within it and not return to an earthly existence. They instantly know it to be better than what they had formerly experienced while in a body. The light feels as natural to a freed soul as water to a fish. It is the doorway to a blissful path. The light beckons the soul forward to a continue life in a grand new way.

It is important that we learn from near death experiences that the light itself is a cleansing force. Within its soothing presence, souls can immediately begin to experience healing from unhappiness, emotional distress, self-condemnation, unworthiness, and many other types of painful suffering. The need for an inner cleansing and healing can also be associated with the third and final major event described within NDEs, the life review. After the disembodied soul meets loved ones and is quickly ushered into the light, these events naturally transition the spirit toward reflection. A life-review of the soul is a personal viewing of one's recent history while on earth. It is like watching an autobiographical movie that retells our past earthly experiences. Usually, the life-review is said to take place in an instant. There is an old adage that best describes this experience.

"My entire life passed before my eyes."

Some may fear that the life-review is a brutal, divine judgment from an angry god, orchestrated only to reveal our past mistakes. I would disagree. Layers upon layers of past experiences are brought to the surface for our benefit. The life-review bears a striking similarity to a Bible passage about revealing what lies hidden within mankind:

Do you bring in a lamp to put it under a bowl or a bed? Instead, don't you put it on its stand? For whatever is hidden is meant to be disclosed, and whatever is concealed is meant to be brought out into the open. - Mark 4:21-22 (NIV)

I think Jesus was declaring that the light within us will reveal any darkness, any secret of untruth we might attempt to bury deep inside our mind. I suspect the cleansing light and life-review that accompanies the death experience is used to reveal the depth of our hearts. It is my conviction that the collective higher consciousness of mankind, which some may view to be God, only works for our good. By having the opportunity to review our past mistakes and triumphs, I would suggest that we are given a great gift. If we are granted the ability to view our past from a higher perspective, then maybe it is easier for us to put it in its proper place. Perhaps, reflection is necessary so we can allow ourselves to move beyond all obstacles. After all, who wants to continually bear the burden of past errors and self-created condemnation? Wouldn't it be much better to be able to relinquish the past so that we are no longer encumbered on our journey? I think this is important if we want to find peace in the present moment.

The common events described within near death experiences, to me, reveal we must undergo a mental cleansing process after our physical bodies expire in order to be free for the journey that lies ahead. After studying a number of these stories, I eventually came to the conclusion that ghosts must be people who were cheated out of this healing, light-experience. While wondering why some spirits might miss out on the cleansing process, I became compassionately aware that such a bright, revealing experience could be wrongly perceived. Lost souls might fear the light, thinking it to be a place of judgment or possibly punishment for past, life choices. Might this explain why some human spirits remain earthbound? I knew deep down that there was not an angry god outside of us who desired retribution for our mistakes. From my own experience, I realize that we are often our own, harshest arbitrator and don't even know it.

If we are beings of light within a collective consciousness, then the light of pure love is the energy inside of every person, and for that matter, within everything. After studying near death experiences, I felt that the light that people have described not only comprised but energized everything that exists. I also suspected that the light was conscious and ever working to bring everything to an awareness of its loving splendor. If light actually resides within us, then ghosts must remain unaware of who they are. Otherwise, why run from the light of one's self?

My curiosity for the ghost condition caused me to wonder how a soul might eventually find the light. Like lost children wanting only to go home, I imagined that ghosts call to us, ever seeking an ear that can hear their cry. If lost spirits truly desired our help, why would they cause peculiar disturbances within the physical environment? What must ghosts be thinking to behave so oddly? The actions of disembodied people seemed quite abnormal when compared to typical human behavior.

Stories about haunting reveal many different sides to ghostly activity. The *Angels & Ghosts* website continued to be a great compliment to my studies. As stories poured in from around the world by way of e-mail, I noticed the accounts of haunting shared common themes that stood out to me. I was very intrigued as I read about ghost behavior. Some people reported feeling cold spots or goose bumps on their skin. Others claimed to have witnessed levitation or the movement of objects, even observing electrical appliances being turned off and on. Some saw shadows that moved. People's pets might behave oddly, such as barking at an empty spot in a room; or fragrances may be detected in the atmosphere of a haunted location. Most often, I received reports of people hearing all sorts of strange noises, such as disembodied footsteps, whispering, music, rapping, banging, something falling to the floor, or doors and drawers creaking. Also, some felt like they were being watched by something they couldn't see. I received reports of many different ghost behaviors, and these were just some of the examples.

There are natural explanations for what some might believe to be paranormal activity; for example, a small animal in a wall or attic could make convincing tapping sounds that normally are not heard within a home. The settling of a house could produce a creaking staircase that alarms us. Perhaps, a drafty residence might allow wind from outside to enter and move some curtains or even cause a person to feel goose bumps. We should also be aware that the unusually high presence of electromagnetic fields or even low-frequency sounds can also create some of this phenomena by producing feelings of anxiety within people's minds. The effect can cause us to sense, hear, and even see things that are not there. Such explanations can be the answer to some of our paranormal encounters but not all of them. Even if normal occurrences within the natural environment account for most of the paranormal experiences people believe they have had, none of these can produce identical hallucinations in multiple witnesses. The most indisputable proof for the existence of ghosts, then, is when two or more people describe seeing the exact same spirit. After examining a wealth of evidence, I became certain that some people truly are seeing and hearing the ghosts of people.

Ghost behavior is considered to be an oddity, a real mystery. It is easy for us to imagine a mischievous specter tip-toeing through our living room, banging on walls, and moving objects just to have a laugh. If ghosts are capable of causing strange disturbances, for what purpose would it serve? I began asking myself this question, because suffering souls certainly wouldn't be trying to have fun at our expense, would they? Some ghosts might find enjoyment in playing tricks upon unsuspecting people, but would we expect every ghost to act in this same manner? People differ from one another, so I was fairly certain this couldn't be the case. I concluded we might have a misconception about ghost behavior. I was nagged by one question.

"Why do ghosts do such odd things?"

When I was a grade-schooler, I can recall going out on Halloween night and playing tricks. Of course, my friends and I also grabbed our share of candy from people, too. We didn't do anything that I would call harmful, though we did throw dried, corn kernels at the front of houses to get people to come to their doors and tossed rolls of toilet paper into people's tree limbs. The folly of youth was upon me in those days, and I remember immediately recounting our adventure to my father. I guess he viewed my activities as harmless fun but made certain to instruct me not to do such things to the elderly. He shared with me that I should "put myself in their shoes." That discussion has stuck with me my entire life. His instruction has become something that I have tried to consistently draw upon when attempting to understand why we, as people, do the things we do.

When I began considering what it must be like to be in the shoes of ghosts, I had a prior incident from which to draw some conclusions; it was my own out-of-body experience. One night while meditating, I was in such a relaxed state that I suddenly floated up and out of my body. To describe it, I was like a pair of eyeballs floating just beneath the ceiling, hovering over my inert form. I could actually see the entire room as I looked down upon it, but I struggled to navigate back to my body due to panic. At first believing I had died, I could only think of how I was not ready to leave my family behind. I wanted to at least be able to say goodbye to family and friends. In fear, I attempted to cry out to my wife who was sleeping in the bed beside my body. Although it sounds odd now, I must have thought that if I could awaken her, and if she in-turn could awaken my body, I might find myself back in it! I tried to scream my wife's name. Nothing came out. Without my body, I didn't have vocal chords to produce a sound. As I fought hard to reach my lifeless shape, I moved toward it ever so slowly. Eventually, my spirit floated back down inside my body, and I regained control of it after a few minutes. Even though the experience only lasted for a short time, I recall being very frightened during the entire event.

When I considered how ghosts must feel, I could not forget how terrified and isolated I felt when my voice had suddenly fallen silent. I was instantly journeying alone, or so it seemed, and my fears quickly took hold of my mind during this unfamiliar episode. While in the midst of my out-of-body experience, I instinctively attempted to summon another's help, in this case my wife. To have had someone who could hear me or even guide me would have been readily welcomed. I recall feeling sad as if my opportunity at life had been lost, wanting so desperately to communicate with my family and friends one more time. Why wouldn't others who were surprised by death's sudden call also feel similar to how I had felt? Ghosts somehow missed the light and greeting from other spirits. They must surely feel alone just like I did. We can easily imagine how they may be afraid, regretful, and desperate to communicate with loved ones. Now capable of comprehending this troubling state, I became certain that ghosts often make noise and cause disturbances in order to attempt to gain our attention. They wish to communicate with the living for a variety of reasons. I speculated that ghosts must have a similar motive, that being fear, for behaving the way that they do.

Can the idea of ghosts wanting help be so far-fetched? After all, science today is proving that what many of us consider our reality is actually an illusion. What we view as being the real world existing outside of ourselves is really only our own personal interpretation. When we see a squirrel sitting atop a fence post, what we are viewing is the mental image of the rodent produced in the back of our brains. The squirrel is simply the brain's interpretation of electrical signals it is receiving from the five senses. Amazingly, our senses detect and interpret energies that are then sent to the brain and transformed into a mental picture. Some quantum physicists are telling us that the squirrel we see, then, is not outside of us but exists as a perception of energy within our mind. They are declaring that the world we believe to be real only exists as a holographic projection within the brain. The energies we see, or may not see in the case of ghosts, only become real to us if we are able to perceive them. Even though we might not be aware of energies such as ghosts and spirits, it does not mean they do not exist. Science is quite possibly on the brink of proving that everything that we consider to be real is actually made up of a greater, invisible energy and interconnected. When one part is affected, the whole is affected as well.

If that concept is not mind-numbing enough, let's consider the idea of parallel universes. For a moment, imagine reality as being made up of different dimensions beyond this physical world. As one, small illustration, *The Time Machine* by H.G. Wells explores the idea of using a sled-like machine to jump back and forth among different periods of human history. The machine itself remains in the exact same location while in operation. History takes place while the observer remains stationary but travels within different dimensions of time. This concept reminded me of the theory that people, and for that matter everything, might possibly have multiple dimensions of existence. Quantum physicists theorize that the world we know might be parallel to, similar to, and in relationship with other universes. I understand this to mean that we potentially exist and interact within other worlds that we currently remain unaware of, even though we are somehow connected to them. Might this possibly explain how disincarnate spirits are able to appear, disappear, and even occasionally interact with people here in this physical realm? This got me thinking. Let us suppose that these parallel dimensions are different planes of our existence. Could different dimensions possibly represent different states of human awareness? If so, I wondered if a simple elevation of awareness would subsequently move a lost soul from one plane unto another.

After my out-of-body experience, I felt strongly that we may walk with others who are immaterial and frequently unperceived. I theorized that maybe due to the overlapping of two worlds, coupled with temporary shifts in our perception, the unseen world momentarily reveals itself to the unsuspecting. Although we may think these different planes of existence collide from time to time, I was wondering if we are unwittingly interacting within both the physical world and other invisible worlds simultaneously. In my first book, I shared a story concerning this concept when I wrote about my son Chad's dream:

I can distinctly recall my younger son sharing a dream with me when he was about eight years old. It was interesting to watch him attempt to convey what he had learned about another plane of existence, what I deem as being the spirit realm. In his dream, he was shown that we interact within multiple realms simultaneously, because we are truly spirits having both a physical and spiritual experience. This revelation was huge for such a young man, and it was not a concept I had previously shared with him. At the time, it seemed coincidental that I had formerly received the same revelation through the spirit within me, but now I realize my son's dream is an awesome confirmation to the voice inside my being.

The idea that we could possibly experience shifts in

awareness, which might give us a glimpse of other worlds, is not an outlandish notion. Most of us live our lives believing that what the brain shows us must be real. Be that as it may, we should still be capable of recognizing the mind's ability to fool us. If we consider human behavior, we may notice that people tend to engage in the habit of time-traveling quite a bit. We often do not recognize when our mind is bound by past events or captivated by imaginations of our future. Although these fabrications may be based upon prior experiences, such thoughts are never the real events themselves. They are based upon memories, illusions generated within our thinking. What I am getting at is if we find ourselves living anywhere but in the present moment, our mind has taken us captive, holding us within a deluded world. The past is a powerful construct of the mind that can appear as real as the present day. Still, we always possess the ability to live our lives within the reality of now or within the illusions of past or future. The choice is invariably ours to make. This is how it is possible for a false perception to become altered in order to gain a new perspective on life.

I became intuitively aware that our ability to create and become trapped within our own illusions of past and future is something that does not necessarily dissipate simply due to death of the physical body. It is a commonly-held belief by many that when a person dies they leave the earth and their former life behind without any strings attached. Due to certain religious teachings, there are those who strongly think that the grave is an impenetrable wall between the quick and the dead. Despite what others choose to believe, it eventually became apparent to me that ghost sightings are evidence that refutes this idea. I could no longer assume that every deceased person progresses directly unto another place. Numerous accounts of disembodied spirits of people, who have remained behind after their physical body expired, reveal that ghosts display a strong attachment to their past, something obviously enforced by the power of their mind. Even though ghosts might not be trapped within a specific, past event, it is certainly prior life experience on earth that still enslaves them. Like many, I felt it was possible for disincarnate spirits to have unfinished business they strongly feel needs to be resolved. Yet, I also suspected some might fear saying goodbye to loved ones, not wanting to face an uncertain future. Even though the reasons for remaining behind on earth likely differ from one ghost to another, I eventually came to the conviction that every ghost is fundamentally living within a false, psychologically-constructed prison. Some are simply lost within their mind more than others. I theorized that ghosts are characteristically haunted by different forms of fear based upon their past experiences, keeping them to some extent disconnected from their own present moment.

I often use the word earthbound spirits to refer to ghosts, but I never intended to imply that the earth literally grips the spirits of troubled people, like a spider's web might contain an unsuspecting insect. Ghosts and haunting are caused by a mental condition. Earthbound, to me, best describes the circumstance of being enchained to a realm and a prior life lived, by the power of one's own psyche. While formulating these ideas, I began to consider more about how we might help ghosts.

"If something is bound, then perhaps it can be unbound," I thought.

As you may have heard, it is an accepted view by many paranormal investigators that ghosts simply have unfinished business to resolve. This could be true. I guess it would depend upon one's definition of "unfinished business." To explore this further, I decided to contemplate a variety of reasons for why a person might stray from the light that usually accompanies the death experience. Following my inner intuition, I theorized that ghosts sometimes choose not to continue their life-journey. I also considered that some spirits may have had little choice in the matter.

From time to time, events happen that we do not expect. This reminds me of the insurance company commercials that tell us, "Life comes at you fast." Death of the physical body may take place anytime or anywhere. Our earthly departure may at any moment catch us completely off-guard, even leaving some unaware of what has happened. A man jogging at night could accidentally be hit by a car from behind, bringing his life here to an end. Might he still be trotting down the street and continuing his daily routine while remaining completely unaware of what has happened? What if a frail woman suffering attack from an assailant loses consciousness due to severe trauma? If she is murdered in the process, will she immediately know what has transpired? Could she remain in a state of shock or find herself disoriented from the tragedy, wandering amongst the living? I suppose it is very possible for a person to die and not be cognizant of it at all.

"How could that be?" you may wonder.

The answer lies in the basis that a spirit does not die. It is impossible. Our accepted idea concerning death is incorrect. Death is only an illusion, for if a person continues to exist even without their body, then the body was never who they really were. If we are truly spirits temporarily living within costumes of flesh, then we can imagine how it might be possible to lose sense of one's person.

People who have experienced a sudden separation from their body still feel alive, much like living in a dream. Their dreamlike state can quickly turn to a nightmare if they have not been lovingly guided toward the light. They may not have noticed their body peel away like the skin from an orange, but eventually they might realize that something is different. It is at this point that a spirit begins to search for answers from the only place they know. They begin to seek help from the living.

Imagine wandering around trying to make sense of a physical world that no longer reacts to you. Are you dreaming? Have you lost your mind? What happened? Your desperate attempt to secure help from family, friends, or anyone else for that matter, falls only upon deaf ears. You feel alive but now need proof of it. No one knows you are around them. Your ability to secure help in order to improve your condition remains in limbo. Some poor ghosts must find themselves continually meandering about in a state of uncertainty.

We can only wonder about the affairs of other ghosts who had their lives stolen from them through violent trauma, such as murder. Intense, emotional distress might have caused their mind to go into shock, quickly shutting down for self-preservation. The buried memory of the horror hides deep inside them, only to be faced at a later date. This degree of inner turmoil could leave a soul staggering hopelessly, not knowing what has happened or where to go. During the times when a portion of the trauma is brought to their remembrance, they might decide to completely disconnect from everything they have ever known. Aiding such a lost soul to overcome their past could prove difficult.

We should also consider the ghosts of those who died during drug abuse, alcohol abuse, or while under medical anesthesia. Might they still be disoriented due to the altering of their mind, lost for a time until able to find their way? I can't help but wonder if the euphoric feeling of mind inhibiting substances, while comfortably transporting people through the dying process, occasionally delivers souls into what must appear to be a no man's land.

After sharing some of my thoughts concerning the fate of lost souls, I do not want you to think that all ghosts are in such a sad state of affairs. Many earthbound spirits are not half-witted zombies strolling around aimlessly. My studies and experiments would soon reveal that many lost spirits understand that their body has died, even knowing they are now considered to be ghosts. It is my purpose to remind people that ghosts are human in thought and action. If we were to search the streets of New York City, I am certain we would find a large number of different personalities that would easily top the number of ice cream flavors found at *Baskin Robbins.* I suspect one could discover people who exemplified the most kind and loving of natures, the darkest and most rotten, and every conceivable variation in-between. My point is that every person is unique: That is what makes everyone relevant and special. Ghosts, like us, are people. I sometimes think we're all just ghosts but with flesh and bone!

Ghosts do differ in personality, behavior, and intentions. Would one expect anything less from a forgotten part of humanity, even though they remain invisible to us in spirit? You might be surprised to learn that ghosts can be happy, sad, protective, and loving. Like us, they can also have a bad day or even choose to be domineering or downright nasty! People are creatures of habit. It is safe to assume that the personalities and behaviors people exhibit will likely remain with them after their physical bodies are gone. If they were negative, they will remain negative until they experience the cleansing power of the light.

I came to expect that ghosts may elect to remain behind with those of us on earth for a myriad of reasons. Some ghosts simply might not know where to go, what to do next, and await somebody's assistance to find their way to the light; however, other ghosts are very much aware of the light but apparently have chosen to reject it. You may wonder why. I already mentioned that some souls fear being punished in Hell for a past deed, and the light could appear to be their time of divine judgment; but some ghosts *know* the light is good. They might not want to face a formerly tough parent whom they fear could be waiting to see them or grandpa who they onetime disappointed. Some ghosts may actually enjoy watching over loved ones or desire to deliver a parting message to an old friend before embracing the light. Eventually, I realized the ghost's choice to remain here must seem very important. Otherwise, why not leave a world behind that can be unkind to the disembodied?

As I worked to further understand these ideas and thoughts that constantly dominated my thinking, I desired to get out in the field and work with live cases of ghosts and haunting. Were my theories correct about the mental conditions of ghosts, and could I effectively help them if my suspicions proved to be true? It was at this point that I began taking additional steps toward answering more of my questions.

Chapter Three

Ghosts in the Machine

During the spring of 2007, I heard an interesting broadcast on the *Coast to Coast* radio program. A man by the name of Frank Sumption and his invention were being discussed by host George Noory and a guest on his show. Frank had created a device dubbed "Frank's Box," a machine that supposedly could bring forth voices of the dead. They played some recordings of ghost messages received from the device. To say the least, I was very intrigued.

After doing a successful search of the Internet, I printed off some schematics that Sumption had provided on-line in the hope of producing my own version of a *Frank's Box*. The "ghost box" was said to work by producing raw audio fragments, coupled with white noise, produced by either a linear or random sweep of an AM or FM tuner. The idea is very similar to taking an old car radio and turning the tuning knob to create a mish-mash of noise from various bits of radio station chatter and the static found in-between stations. Tangled within this audio noise is where the ghost voices were said to be found. Frank Sumption had created a unique way to make a tuner continually sweep the AM and FM bands. He also built some additional enhancements into his device.

Frank's Box is the original ghost box, with each model being hand-built by Sumption on his work bench. Although his designs always vary, they work by generating raw audio bits and white noise, utilizing an AM or FM tuner. This set-up can enhance the clarity and sheer number of ghost messages received. Sumption conceived of the idea by experimenting with Stefan Bion's *EVPmaker* software that is used to record spirit voices utilizing a computer. He was also inspired by an October 1995 *Popular Electronics* magazine article that asked, "Are the dead trying to communicate with us through electronic means? Try these experiments and see for yourself." Soon, Frank began building what would eventually become his unique and controversial ghost box design.

Frank Sumption maintains that the entities use bits of speech, music, and noise produced by the ghost box in order to form audible voices. He asserts that these communications often contain specific words pulled from different radio broadcasts that are then used to create a meaningful message. Sumption has also taken note of an entity's ability to manipulate signals and voltages, finding this phenomenon difficult to comprehend. He believes that most of this sound manipulation occurs inside the electronics of the ghost box. In addition, it is his opinion that some entities may transmit a signal that can be carried through the boxes. Frank Sumption still continues to investigate this field out of curiosity, remaining intrigued by the ghost box voices he hears and records that shouldn't be there.

The idea of recording the voices of ghosts is certainly not new, often being referred to as electronic voice phenomena by ghost investigators. There has been quite a lot of documented evidence to support the existence of electronic voice phenomena, also known as "EVP" for short. The idea of otherworldly communication can be traced back as early as 1889 when inventor Nikola Tesla discovered he was receiving mysterious transmissions from his radio tower. Even though Tesla thought that these transmissions were evidence of interplanetary communication, it is important to note that he remained convinced that the disturbances were not the product of terrestrial origin:

Others may scoff at this suggestion or treat it as a practical joke, but I have been in deep earnest about it ever since I made the first observations at my wireless plant in Colorado Springs from 1889 to 1900. At the time I carried on those investigations there existed no wireless plant on the globe other than mine, at least none that could produce a disturbance perceptible in a radius of more than a few miles. Furthermore, the conditions under which I operated were ideal, and I was well trained for the work." - Nikola Tesla, Sept. 24, 1921, excerpted from his letter *Interplanetary Communication*

Another inventor, Thomas Edison, was very interested in after-death communication. In the 1920s, it is documented that he attempted to invent a device to communicate with the dead.

"If our personality survives, then it is strictly logical or scientific to assume that it retains memory, intellect, other faculties, and knowledge that we acquire on this Earth. Therefore, if we can evolve an instrument so delicate as to be affected by our personality as it survives in the next life, such an instrument, when made available, ought to record something." – Thomas Alva Edison

Although Edison was unsuccessful in producing a machine

that could communicate with the dead, the discovery of mysterious voices being heard while using electronic devices occurred as early as the 1930s. A phonograph and a vacuum tube radio were two early pieces of equipment reported to have brought forth voices of the deceased by different experimenters. In 1952, the first EVP was accidentally recorded by two Catholic priests using a magnetophone. The 1960s brought forth two men in particular who worked diligently to record disembodied voices and document their findings. The first to do this was Friedrich Juergenson..

As the legend goes, in 1959 the Swedish film producer was out recording bird calls when he could hear his deceased mother's voice speaking to him upon playback of the audio tape. This led to Juergenson experimenting and, over time, recording hundreds of ghost voices. Having authored books about his discoveries, he is now considered to be the "Father of EVP."

Fascinated by the work of Juergenson, Latvian psychologist Dr. Konstantin Raudive began his own EVP experiments. He would eventually record and study thousands of disembodied voices, creating a system of classification for electronic voice phenomena in order to rate the quality and clarity of the messages.

Following the discovery of EVP, various methods and machines were developed to attempt to enhance communication with ghosts. The one device that would become of special significance to me was, of course, Frank Sumption's ghost box.

The thought of two-way communication with ghosts and

spirits through the use of electronic devices intrigued me. As someone who had enjoyed reading the book *Ghosts* by Hans Holzer, I was fascinated by the idea of speaking with the dead. In his book, Holzer recounts experience after experience of investigating haunted locations utilizing his select group of skilled psychic-mediums. Each medium was able to allow disembodied spirits to speak through them using the medium's own vocal chords. Holzer was careful to record detailed notes about these sessions. Together, Hans Holzer and his psychic investigators worked hard to communicate with ghosts, assisting them whenever possible.

I couldn't help but think that a new electronic tool, such as the ghost box, might be a huge breakthrough in ghost communication. Can you imagine the possibilities if we could carry on conversations with people on the other side of the grave? I became very determined to keep track of the development of this device until I could figure out a way to make or acquire one for myself.

By early December 2007, word came to me about an abbreviated method used to create a simplified version of Frank's ghost box. Someone, who at the time wished to remain anonymous, had discovered he could buy an AM/FM radio off the shelf at *Radio Shack*, disassemble it, clip a wire, and cause it to sweep both the AM and FM frequencies. It produced raw audio bits and white noise similar to Frank's ghost box. After making his discovery known, a few people tried using this version of the ghost box to capture spirit voices. They found it worked quite well. This type of ghost box became known as the "Radio Shack hack." Eventually, it would make its way into the hands of many paranormal investigators.

Upon hearing about this breakthrough, I rushed out to my local *Radio Shack* store, picked up several different radios, and began altering them for experimental purposes. I ran all sorts of tests in an attempt to enhance the noise generated by the devices. In order to identify the best method to record the voices of ghosts, I also made numerous recordings of the raw audio noise. After experimenting with a wide-array of set-ups, I finally concluded that my best opportunity to capture messages from ghosts would be to simply lay a small audio recorder beside the radio's speaker.

As I recorded the audio, I began listening to the words coming out of the sweeping tuner's speakers. I was hoping to hear a message that might make sense to me, something that would verify that the ghost box could be used to communicate with ghosts. Occasionally, I might hear a word or two through the speakers while recording the audio. I admit that I struggled to hear anything live. Whether I heard a message through the speakers, or not, was not very important to me. I had chosen to rely more upon listening with headphones to the recorded audio files that I had downloaded to my computer afterward; this way, I could analyze the audio more fully. Admittedly, I was skeptical about the ghost box, especially when my initial results seemed fruitless.

The first event of significance occurred in my dining room. It caused me to begin to think that Frank Sumption possibly stumbled upon something incredible. I turned on the *Radio Shack* ghost box, and in the midst of its sweep, I heard my name come through the speaker.

"Purely coincidental," I reasoned. "It's going to take more than that to convince me. Should I be asking this thing questions?"

A few minutes later, I clearly heard my wife's name. "Another coincidence," I again thought. Within 10 seconds, the phone rang and my wife was on the other end of the line. It was then that I corrected myself for being so critical and close-minded.

"Perhaps, I better keep experimenting," I said to myself under my breath. It was an interesting experience, one that I needed to compel me to continue working with electronic ghost communication.

When listening to the ghost box sweep a radio band, it is possible to detect quite a bit of radio chatter from disc jockeys and music being played. It was important for me to decide what criteria should be used to determine if a message was from a ghost or spirit, something distinct from snippets of radio broadcasts. I decided that I would ask questions while the device was turned on and then wait for relative responses. If I should receive answers that were specific to my questions, then it would make sense that something intelligent was coming forth through the ghost box. I would try to stay away from questions that only required a "yes" or "no" as answers. If ghosts were communicating, then it would make sense they could give us something significant and specific as a response. Also, answers in the form of longer phrases would be much better evidence. I chose to eliminate one-word replies whenever possible. If they were possibly relevant, then I would accept them. This would make it much more difficult for radio broadcasts to be mistaken as legitimate communication from ghosts.

Some who have worked with ghost box communication believe that ghosts and spirits are able to manipulate the raw audio and white noise to form words. After my experiments, I do not subscribe to that theory. Many of the recorded messages I captured seem to ride on top of the ghost box noise, as if the raw audio forms a carrier wave capable of bringing forth the thoughts of the ghost or spirit that wishes to communicate. My theory actually corresponds nicely with certain methods for recording EVP. Ghost investigators sometimes create noise while attempting to record electronic voice phenomena. They believe it helps them to capture more spirit voices. It is well known in the field of *Instrumental Transcommunication* (the use of electronic devices to contact spirits) that the use of a fan, running water, or a white noise generator can enhance the ability to record EVP. I have also noticed during ghost investigations that EVPs often seem to be recorded while people are talking. It's as if the sound of human speech produces the perfect carrier wave to bring forth the voices of disembodied spirits. Sometimes, these mysterious messages will be heard over top of people in the room as they talk. I suspect the ghost box functions in a similar manner; however, I still am not certain how the ghost box actually works. I only know I have recorded some amazing messages that I find difficult to discount to chance.

Some of the first voices I recorded were from spirits, not earthbound ghosts; their messages were enlightened. In fact, I might say these voices even encouraged me in this endeavor. The more I used the ghost box, the more the frequency of communications improved. Starting out, I felt lucky to record one message; but this soon changed. After a couple weeks of experimenting, every time I turned the device on I would hear my name and receive excellent, relevant responses to my questions. It was as if an expectation had been established with those who were interested in communicating with me.

I conducted short recording sessions of only a couple minutes at a time. Longer recordings became cumbersome to analyze, so I preferred to review shorter recordings for messages. As the connection with spirits increased, I felt impressed that I should ask these enlightened beings about helping ghosts. In metaphysical circles, the idea of aiding ghosts is often referred to as "spirit rescue." I put forth my questions about this topic while using the ghost box.

"Is spirit rescue the goal (for me to learn while working with the ghost box)?" I asked.

"Please, it is very important...very important. Yes," I recorded.

The response I heard sounded like a deep, male voice that became higher pitched and feminine sounding. This was strange.

"Was more than one spirit communicating with me?" I wondered.

I theorized that perhaps the raw audio itself might be changing the pitch of the spirit messages and so I tried not to think of the words as originating from either a male or female spirit. Gender was not important. It was the answers that I was after.

"What can you tell me about spirit rescue?" I blurted out to the ghost box.

"Everything. It's possible."

To say the least, I was very encouraged by the exchange of relevant responses to my questions. Something or someone was now urging me forward on my quest to help ghosts, and it mirrored the messages I had been hearing inside me during meditation.

I still had it in my mind that I needed to test the audio of different ghost box set-ups even though I had already recorded a message through the ghost box that seemed impatient.

"You're testing this forever!"

When I heard this recording, I chuckled. "Impatient spirits, aren't they?" I thought.

Still, I decided to make six more 20 second recordings of different ghost box configurations. During these tests, I recorded a distinctly clear and powerful spirit message.

"The earth...they need...our work."

I was shocked when I heard these powerful words surface during playback of my test audio session. The spirit voice slowly emphasized this message over a span of about six seconds, making it impossible to have originated from one radio station. In fact, the altered radio I was using required about ten seconds to completely sweep the entire FM band. According to the *Federal Communications Commission* website, the FM band is divided into 100 channels. This would mean my radio, now converted into a spirit communicator, passed over approximately ten channels per second. The six second spirit message was captured while the ghost box swept through approximately 60 channels; therefore, the lengthy spirit communication was certainly not a quick radio blurb. The odds would be near impossible that the phrase was created from different radio station broadcasts, especially when the voice was consistent the entire way through the recording. The pitch of it never changed. Furthermore, I could hear it over top of the noise generated by the sweeping radio as if it were an EVP. Later, I would hear in another recording that I made that this ghost box message came from my spirit guide.

During another ghost box recording session, I decided to ask more questions regarding ghosts.

"Are there a lot of earthbound spirits?"

"Yes. Hell. So many different spirits here..."

"Can we call on a deceased love one?" I questioned.

"Yes." I decided to allow this one-word answer, as the other communications were lengthy and relevant.

I wanted to know if the ghost box could be used to help ghosts, so I asked, "Can ghosts be brought forth through you guys?"

"Sure..." I needed more information. It was another one-word reply but possibly relevant. I would consider it for now.

As my experiments and questions continued daily through

early 2008, I had decided to use a contact I have in the toy industry in order to see if we could build our own, unique ghost box. Sharing the recent find of the *Radio Shack* hacks, my friend was very interested in attempting to construct a prototype from the Frank's Box schematics. Knowing people who build prototypes for toy concepts, he contacted a gentleman who quickly built a simple, but very different, version of the ghost box. I couldn't wait to receive the test model to experiment with it.

My work continued with the *Radio Shack*-type ghost boxes in the meantime. My questions concerning the condition of ghosts and spirits weighed heavily on my mind. It showed in my experimentation.

"What is the message the world needs?" I queried.

"Ghosts speak..." I heard this message multiple times in this recording, obviously for emphasis.

In another session I asked, "(Are there) any spirits of the light who wish to speak?"

I heard the short response, "Me."

"How do we help murder victims?"

"Say it. Murdered," came the reply to my question.

Was I to let the dead know they had died? I wondered. After this interesting response, I struggled to hear more communication. It was time to conclude my session for that day.

By late February of the same year, I received the prototype ghost box from the electronics expert who resides in California. I was shocked that it did not take very long to construct. At first glance, it looked amazing; but I was unsure of how to operate it. Turning it on, the sounds it made initially disappointed me.

"No wonder it arrived to me so quickly. It's not made correctly," I surmised.

Although I was a bit disheartened, this new ghost box did have more features to play with than a simple *Radio Shack* hack. The prototype operated differently than most other sweeping radios I had read about. It worked by a linear scan of the FM band, jumping from strongest signal to strongest signal. Because its sound was different, producing more radio snippets and less white noise, I was initially pessimistic. Still, the prototype allowed me to make some fantastic tuning adjustments. Not only could I choose the specific region of the FM band that the device would scan but also set the speed of its operation. I would soon discover that our experimental ghost box was capable of bringing forth some of the clearest ghost messages I had ever recorded.

I shoved the device into a box and took it to my friend Walt's apartment. Working together, we adjusted the settings and listened to the raw audio. The more we remained patient with testing the prototype, the better it appeared to be working. Initially, I heard both my name and the name of my wife come through the device.

"That was sounding familiar," I thought.

As I adjusted the rate of the sweep several times, I recorded a very relevant message concerning my penchant for continually turning the various knobs. It was perfect confirmation that the prototype worked.

"Hold rate. Sweep through."

Instantly, I knew that I was to quit adjusting the sweeping rate and allow the prototype to function at the current settings. Communication was definitely occurring, and I knew it. Then, I recorded a response that encouraged me even more.

"I said he heard it. Yeah, he did."

Whoever was speaking through the device was talking to someone other than Walt and me, affirming that we had heard the message about holding the rate of sweep. It was interesting to eavesdrop on spirits communicating with one another. I had to cut this initial session short that day but continued experimenting with the prototype as often as possible.

During my next session of experimentation, I asked, "Will this (ghost box) model work for spirit rescue?"

The response was quite remarkable. "Clear. Yes. Hey..." The voice trailed off.

"Say that, again?" I asked.

"Good for spirits," was the reply. At this point, I had become certain that I had acquired an electronic device that would allow me to hear ghosts and spirits.

It was time to test the ghost box out with ghosts. Up to this point, the communications I was receiving seemed enlightened. What I mean by this is that the spirits who were being heard through the device were not in need of my help. Actually, I had been in need of *their* assistance. The messages received from spirits had provided invaluable confirmation of my ideas.

What was I following, and why was I doing this? Sometimes, I was not sure but knew I seemed to have little choice in the matter. I could have stopped, I suppose; but my higher consciousness compelled me forth in this venture. When I reflect upon these events now, it is fair to say I was not at peace unless I continued down the path that kept unfolding before me. I was driven to experiment with the ghost box. Even when I had forgotten about the initial radio broadcast concerning Frank Sumption's device, I was somehow reminded to check back into it six months later. This was only a few days after the *Radio Shack* hack discovery had surfaced. It seems my thoughts were not my own. Someone unseen to me was making sure I embarked down this path. I knew I was to work with ghost communication, and there was no running away from it.

As I sought more ways to test my developing theories regarding ghosts and spirits, another friend of mine had recently lost his mother to cancer near the time I had received the ghost box prototype. He had been aware of my experiments and wanted me to try and reach his mother through the device. I agreed to do so and was startled by some of the results I recorded in an upstairs bedroom of his home.

When I first arrived there, he told me of a possible sighting of an apparition. My friend suspected the former owner might still roam the upstairs hallway. We agreed it might be a good idea to first attempt to reach the man of the house. My friend began the questioning.

"Is Samuel still here?"

"Help. He isn't," was the response. The communication was quick and concise.

"Are there any other spirits here?" I questioned, now taking the lead.

"Yes. Help us to talk to our kids," was the response I would later hear on the recording.

"Can you give us the names of any ghosts that are here?" I asked.

"Helen and Audrey."

Helen was the name of my friend's mom. This was excellent confirmation, but who was Audrey? Later, I realized that this could be my grandmother who I never had the chance to meet. She died of cancer when my mother was only 13 years old, well before I was born. It seemed more than coincidence that she had fallen victim to the same disease as my friend's mom. Was my grandmother with me to help her? I had to wonder. Now, when I look at my notes from the experiments I made over the years, I noticed I had recorded the name Audrey numerous times. It was as if she had been assisting me to help other women in spirit.

We continued our questioning some more in the small bedroom, and I took more specific direction from my friend. He had explained to me between sessions that the death of his mother had caused a major riff of some sort between him and his siblings. He and his sister were at odds with the younger brother.

So, I asked, "What should they do about their brother?"

"Help them to be happy with me," was the response. My friend received his mother's instruction, and hopefully she found peace through being able to deliver her last wish to her son. Afterward, I encouraged him to speak to his sister and mend fences with their brother.

Some of these responses were heard in real time during the session at my friend's house; however, all of them were captured by my audio recorder. It was a custom of mine to analyze my recordings of each ghost box session to be sure I didn't miss anything. Headphones and the ability to repeatedly listen to the audio files helped me greatly. In this case, I would later hear multiple pleas for help on the recording that I found disturbing.

When I first began recording ghost box messages, I didn't realize cries for help would become prevalent. As I continued my experiments with the ghost box and became aware of the desperate pleas, I felt passionate toward communicating with hurting spirits. The more I did so, the more I noticed cries for help within the audio files. It became quite common for me to hear and record "help," "help me," or "help us" almost every time I turned on the ghost communication tool. It was as if word went out that spirit voices could be heard by me. Someone other than me was listening. Was I becoming more attuned to hearing their cries, or were ghosts who needed my assistance being brought to me by enlightened spirits? My continued experiments would help to answer these questions.

Chapter Four

Into the Field We Go

The messages I received from the ghost box confirmed what I had known for many years. My websites were full of deeper thought about ghosts and spirit, much of which I learned from listening to the voice that speaks deep within my person. When I write about this voice, allow me to say that all of us have it, though we may not recognize its timbre.

The voice does not differ in any way from what a Christian might deem as being the Holy Spirit or what a psychic might call intuition. To me, such labels are created through different experiences, each a personal interpretation that can simply be boiled down to semantics. I find it common for people to occasionally follow what they call a "gut feeling." It's all the same to me. If a person can learn to silence their head, the voice will be heard within. It is a part of everyone.

I was compelled within me to put pieces of the puzzle together about lost spirits; therefore, I felt it necessary to become involved with as many ghost investigations as possible. If I were to prove my ideas concerning the condition of ghosts and how we could help them, I would need to get my hands dirty by experimenting more out in the field. This led me to becoming an active member of a couple paranormal investigative groups.

I also embarked upon additional, personal excursions in order to satisfy my thirst for answers. It is very safe to assume, that for a time, my work in this field had utterly consumed me.

After initially being rejected by a local group close to my home, I was fortunate to be acquainted with a psychic-medium by the name of Laura Lyn. Laura was a member of a newly formed ghost investigation team that went by the name of *SIGHT*, an acronym for "Spiritual Insight Ghost Hunting Team." After hearing of my struggles to find a group that would allow me to experiment, Laura had insisted I become a part of the team. My tests in haunted locations quickly ensued, eventually giving me many fascinating stories to tell.

I wanted to reveal my ideas about ghost communication to the small Akron, Ohio paranormal group. An opportunity presented itself right away. Once a month, *SIGHT* would have a meeting at an alleged haunted location, and the event was open to anyone who wished to come. They came to be known as *SIGHT* "Mystery Nights." The great thing about these Mystery Nights was that the owners or caretakers of the haunted properties would often give us a tour and allow us to investigate. This provided excellent opportunities for me to test out the ghost box prototype unhindered.

A most remarkable experience with the ghost box occurred on a *SIGHT* Mystery Night up in Fairport Harbor, Ohio. The recordings from that evening would not only astound me and group members but guests who also came to take part in the event. We collectively heard live responses from spirits through the ghost box speaker. These were stunning, interactive communications from ghosts that I thankfully recorded for later review.

Into the Field We Go

Our night began at the *Chef Fritz Roadhouse*, a small, notoriously-haunted bar in this quiet town. The owner of the place seemed quite alright with the activity and openly welcomed discussion of it. At the time, I must admit that I was completely unaware of its haunted history. "Mike," as we called him, shared numerous stories about the bar's past. He also showed us ghost photographs taken within the old watering hole. Initially, I found myself being skeptical of Mike's stories.

"Yeah, sure it is haunted," I thought to myself, "a great way to drum up business."

The old town of Fairport Harbor, Ohio is interesting, because it is an old port on Lake Erie. In its early years, visitors often passed through the town. Bars were opened to vie for travelers' business. The building that houses *Chef Fritz* was likely built well before 1900. It is rumored to have once been a gentlemen-only establishment. A urine trough conveniently located by the bar allegedly kept thirsty patrons drinking almost non-stop. Sailors were said to have visited the place regularly, and legend has it that the upstairs had become home to a brothel.

There are many ghost stories associated with the bar's notorious past. The owner, Mike, believes that the ghosts that haunt *Chef Fritz* are either former employees or patrons. He told us the story of a prostitute named Mary who had been raped and murdered upstairs, her body being tossed in the nearby river. A former madam is also believed to watch over the upstairs area above the old bar. Mike affectionately calls her

"Mary Mae." Could Mary Mae still be caring for her ladies of ill repute?

Two more ghosts are said to haunt *Chef Fritz*. One, a constable, seems to enjoy Mike's company and the hospitality of *Chef Fritz*. Mike learned he was shot and killed in the bar area about a century ago. Mike also told us of another ghost that he labeled as being a "dark spirit" that haunts the basement area. I remember seeing a photo of a black mist coming up the steps from the basement while there. This ghost is negative in nature, according to Mike, and someone he claims to have physically wrestled with at times. Although a couple other ghosts were mentioned, these are the primary spirits of note that are said to haunt the *Chef Fritz Roadhouse*.

As the *SIGHT* Mystery Night progressed, I made my way to the landing of the steps that led to the upstairs. I had been drawn to that area, compelled by just a feeling within me. As I turned on the ghost box prototype for the first time, the help messages began almost at once. After a few minutes of recording, I came down the stairs and into the bar area. As I was talking with another member of *SIGHT* about the landing area, I felt a presence come upon me. It felt like tingles that all of a sudden came out of nowhere.

"What just happened?" I asked my friend with a dumbfounded face.

Laura Lyn saw my expression and came over.

"Did you see the older lady that just whizzed past you?" she asked. I had not seen anything.

Into the Field We Go

After these experiences, I was convinced that *Chef Fritz* was a true, active haunting. I had decided to get back up the stairs to the landing and make some more recordings. Others, having become aware that something had just happened to me, followed me up the stairs. Immediately, we could hear voices coming through the spirit communicator that seemed to be talking with us! It is not uncommon for me to have to review the audio later with headphones to be able to hear the quick communications, but this night was very different. As we began asking questions, we heard intelligent responses that were specific to the conversation.

We felt the spirits at *Chef Fritz* were very active and desiring to communicate with us. As we worked to hear their pleas, it became evident to everyone that there were ghosts of people there who wanted our help. Their cries seemed so desperate as if they were lost and trapped within their own emotional turmoil. It made me sad to think that there could be people around us that are unseen, hurting and desperate to gain our attention. My sadness motivated me to question their condition.

"Do you need help?"

"Many stuck at Fritz," came through the audio.

Laura Lyn then jumped into the questioning while the rest of us listened.

"Can you tell us if there's somebody here that was ever hurt? If you are hurt, please tell us."

"I need help," was the response that we together heard through the prototype. I also thought I heard someone say the word "rape," but was unsure.

"Someone here thought they heard the word 'rape.' Did someone here get raped?" Laura asked.

"Raped." All of us heard this response to the question. The communications back and forth were amazingly simple but precise.

Laura wondered about the former madam, Mary. "Is this Mary or someone else here with us?"

"Mary," crackled through the speaker. Whoever this was repeated the word as if to confirm.

"Mary, do you protect this place...protect the women?" Laura focused her question even more to what she thought she perceived was happening within *Chef Fritz*.

"I, alone." We wondered if this response meant that Mary was still taking care of the brothel that no longer existed in this building. Could she somehow be trapped in the past? Around this time, we heard another message through the ghost communicator. This caused the conversation to change.

"Different spirits...spirits," popped out of the noisy radio suddenly.

"What? Who is here?" I jumped back in to lead the questioning.

"Patrick. Help her." I wondered who Patrick was and his role here at the bar. Was he a former patron? I didn't know. Was he trying to help the other spirits or was he also a lost soul wandering this place?

As we worked to receive more information through the

ghost box prototype at *Chef Fritz*, some of the women who were witnessing the communication began sensing they were suddenly being touched inappropriately by an unseen entity. A male voice spoke through the ghost box prototype and attempted to explain his actions. It appeared he was a mischievous ghost whose behavior had upset a person in the group. She began questioning him out loud.

"What's going on with this game?"

"Your body." This caused the small group to gasp in surprise to the response.

"Your body? Why do you have to be so nasty! We're just here to find out why you're here," the lady said, scolding the ghost.

"Playful," was the next response. The ghost box seemed to be working almost like a walkie-talkie. The real-time, two-way discussion continued.

"Playful?" The group repeated in unison the reply we heard come through the ghost box.

"Yeah," offered the ghost as confirmation to our question.

"Do you have any messages? This is your last chance," someone said to the male ghost.

"Spirits want free." This was a difficult message to hear, for we knew that we did not have permission to help the ghosts during our visit. Also, our time to leave the small bar had come upon us. The events of that evening certainly gave us an experience that we would not soon forget. I am sure that most of us who listened to the exchanges between the living and the dead were astonished that night.

These events that took place at the *Chef Fritz Roadhouse* were beneficial in my work to understand the mind of the ghost. It seems that some ghosts do indeed have intentions to interact with the living in ways that may be perceived as negative at times. After all, ghosts are just people without physical bodies. It is not surprising, then, that the personalities, motives, and desires of lost spirits do not differ much from when they walked the earth. I guess some ghosts do have a sense of humor.

After our experience that night, I not only wondered how many ghosts might be trapped there at *Chef Fritz* due to prior emotional trauma, but how many may remain there in an attempt to satisfy various addictions or vices from the past. Were some of the troubled spirits former alcoholics? The questions filled my mind, but it was time to move to our next location that was awaiting our arrival, *The Fairport Harbor Lighthouse & Museum*.

There's something about a lighthouse that can often evoke thoughts of tragedy at sea or of a lonely light keeper living in isolation away from the local community. Unlike many lighthouses, the *Fairport Harbor Lighthouse* was not isolated from the town. It sits on the shore of Lake Erie at the edge of the small village.

Being constructed in 1825, the original light tower and keeper's house rapidly fell into a state of disrepair. The house and tower were completely built anew in 1871 due to the former buildings' severe deterioration. This building and tower still stand today, though it was abandoned in 1925 when the *West*

Breakwater Lighthouse was erected out in the harbor.

The haunted *Fairport Harbor Lighthouse* and keeper's home is now home to the *Fairport Marine Museum.* It was the first lighthouse and grounds to be restored and converted into a museum within the continental United States. Dedicated in 1945, the museum stands as a monument to the history of the lighthouse, something that Fairport Harbor residents believe should not be forgotten.

The night we visited, the museum caretakers told us the history of the lighthouse. There were two prominent light keepers in its history. The very first lighthouse keeper was Samuel Butler. Being a firm abolitionist, he succeeded in making the *Fairport Harbor Lighthouse* into a northern terminal of the *Underground Railroad.* It was a brilliant way to safely guide runaway slaves to the safety of Canada, which lies just across the Great Lakes.

The second lighthouse keeper of note was Captain Joseph Babcock. He was the first keeper of the reconstructed lighthouse and home. Being fond of his duty at the new lighthouse, Captain Babcock raised his family on the grounds. Both of his children were born in the home, with one of them dying at the young age of five years old from smallpox.

The tragedy of losing the boy at such a young age was bad enough to endure, but then Mrs. Babcock also fell ill and remained bedridden inside the home. It is said she kept many cats to help provide her company while her husband tended the lamp and grounds. Long after Mrs. Babcock's death, some claimed to have seen the spirit of a cat whisking up and down the home's stairs. The ghost cat has been described as resembling a gray puff of smoke. An eerie, mummified cat, which now remains on display in the museum, was later found by a repairman in an upstairs crawl space. Could this be the body of the cat that haunts the keeper's house?

After our previous experience that same night at *Chef Fritz Roadhouse* down the street, we were eager to see what we might record in the lighthouse and keeper's home. I first began asking questions at the top of the lighthouse tower while the ghost box was in operation.

"Where's Captain Butler?"

"Spirit." The reply resonated within the small tower, being clearly discernible through the ghost box.

"Who's on duty as the keeper?" I continued.

"Captain Bruce Nelson." I had not heard of this man and knew there wasn't anyone in charge of operating this lighthouse. It was not an active light any longer. Later, I would do some research and find out the former director of the *Great Lakes Lighthouse Keepers Association* bore this same name. The *GLLKA* is dedicated to preserving lighthouses and their history. It seemed to be an interesting coincidence, especially knowing that lighthouse keepers often bore the title of captain. Bruce Nelson had certainly been in charge of keeping lighthouses. Did that make him a captain of sorts? I wondered. After this, I then made my way down the spiraling metal stairs and into the keeper's house.

The upstairs bedroom of the home had some interesting history and I surmised that maybe a ghost or two could be found there. After I made my way up to the second floor, I was greeted by many of our group who also had wanted to explore the bedroom of the late Mrs. Babcock. I switched on the ghost box prototype, and the group took turns asking questions. I was a little disappointed as the device did not seem to pick up much of anything while in the house. It operated differently from previous sessions I had conducted that same evening. When I examined the recordings the next day, I was surprised to hear the following exchange take place within the home.

"Is there a Captain Babcock here?" someone asked.

"Babcock" quickly blurted out on the recording. I had to slow it down to hear it more clearly.

"Is there any ghosts around here?" one lady was heard asking on the audio.

"Spirit of Babcock." This reply was surprisingly distinct and clear, being spoken with emphasis.

I was shocked at the sheer number of intelligent, two-way conversations that took place that evening. I found it difficult to disprove these communications as being merely coincidence. If the replies to our questions had been insignificant, one-word responses, I might not have continued my experiments. I not only heard relevant answers, but at times there were remarkable phrases that demonstrated what the ghosts were thinking. It would be impossible for me to discount such evidence even though the ghost box method might be considered by some to be controversial.

Soon after my Fairport Harbor experiences, I had an idea. I wanted to communicate with more ghosts who were suffering. What better place to study the mind and condition of ghosts than to visit a former mental institution? If ghosts truly linger in such locations, one would assume that it wouldn't be their first choice of habitation in most cases. I couldn't help but wonder why a poor spirit would actually want to haunt a graveyard or abandoned building. Such behavior suggested to me that when ghosts haunt unattractive locations, they unwittingly choose to do so. Some may remain unaware that they have made a choice to haunt. It is possible they want to leave but are unable to do so. The haunting of frightening locations is most likely due to disturbed minds unfortunately becoming trapped in time and place within our plane of existence. Consequently, I theorized that a former mental health facility, or even a cemetery, might provide plenty of specters in a variety of deplorable states. Those who wanted to leave would be searching for a way out. It was lost spirits, such as these, that I wanted to attempt to communicate with and hopefully help. Maybe, I could present a way out of their prison, so to speak. For if I could speak to the mentally traumatized and find some success, then I could assume that just about anyone who was trapped on the other side of the grave could be rescued.

I knew of a haunted, former mental institution that was not far away from where I lived. It provided me with expansive grounds I could wander and probably not be bothered. Even better, I would not need permission to explore the property. Although I would not have access to the inside of the buildings, would it really matter? I felt only the mind could confine a spirit to a place, not the walls of brick and mortar. This would be a great location to continue experimenting with ghost communication.

Located in northeast Ohio's Stark County, *Massillon State Hospital* opened its doors to psychiatric patients in 1898. It was constructed as a series of castle-like buildings that have been rumored to connect to one another by way of underground tunnels. During its heyday as a hospital for the mentally insane, it is said to have housed close to 3000 patients. Today the old hospital is mostly abandoned even though a newer psychiatric care facility shares part of its grounds.

For years, the old mental hospital has been a source for local lore about its haunting. Almost everyone I have ever talked to about *Massillon State*, especially those who have worked within its buildings, have a story to share about the spirited phenomena that takes place there. I don't believe I could have chosen a better site to continue my next set of experiments. At the time, I kept thinking to myself, "This is the place."

I first wanted to test the ghost box prototype during daylight hours on the hospital grounds while alone. Nobody would accompany me, and I welcomed the break from a group setting. It was a sunny, warm summer day. As I walked the old hospital property I felt nothing unusual. In an attempt to remain discreet, I elected to make my recordings within a small portico on the west side of the McKinley building. The concrete entranceway allowed me to be less visible to any employees that might drive by from the newer behavioral hospital down the road. I wasn't trespassing, but I didn't want to be interrupted.

I was very excited at the thought of turning on the ghost communicator and could only imagine what I might hear. I mentioned that I made my initial visit during daytime. This was part of the experiment, for I wondered how this might affect ghost communication. My goal was to have a successful first outing by possibly making contact with former mental patients. Would there be a high quantity of quality messages from spirits, or would daylight drive some ghosts into hiding? I couldn't wait to find out. I switched on the communicator and listened intently.

"Help."

"Did I hear help?" I wondered aloud. The quick response surprised me just a bit.

"Help." I could also swear I heard the words "medical facility" and "doctor," but I wasn't certain.

As my mind contemplated what I thought I had heard, I elected, for some reason, to move to the north sidewalk of the same building. Again, I turned the ghost box prototype on but remained just a bit tense as I noticed some people walking down a sidewalk nearby.

"Help me. Help me," permeated the nervous air.

I was certain this time that I was repeatedly hearing messages of help. This was not radio chatter. I deduced that the voices must have been ghosts, for their begging cries were clearly heard by me. How could I ignore their lowly pleas from a veiled realm? Still, I wanted to remain objective. Even though I wished to stay and experiment more, I became distracted by men nearing my location. They were obviously on break from undergoing judge-mandated counseling sessions at a recovery center that was housed in one of the buildings. I felt it was time to head back home.

"I heard your requests for help. I promise to come back and help you," I offered.

No matter what the reason, I still felt badly about leaving. I knew I had to return and at least attempt to answer these cries that had come to my attention. We had not been able to assist the ghosts at *Chef Fritz*, and this had left me feeling cold and callous. I didn't want to feel this way again. How many years have some of these spirits begged for mercy? Have others allowed the ghosts' desperate requests to fall upon deaf ears? Questions filled my head about the day's events. My ghost investigations had awakened me to something important but not recognized by many paranormal investigators. I concluded that my return visit would be more focused toward helping some of the ghosts stranded at *Massillon State Hospital*.

On the way home, I decided to steer my small SUV into *Massillon Cemetery*. I was still bothered by the fact that, being comfortable with recording enlightened spirits, now I was repeatedly capturing the voices of suffering ghosts. The communications I initially recorded with the ghost box were not fearful or desperate like the words I heard through the speaker while at *Chef Fritz* or *Massillon State*. This made me consider the possibility that maybe the ghost box messages we record can sometimes be a mixture of ghost and spirit voices. Incorporeal communications don't have to be from one or the other. If unseen spirits and ghosts are interacting with us in a shared energy, why wouldn't both desire to speak with us if possible? It would make sense that we should be able to record messages from both ghosts and spirits; therefore, I decided to welcome any and all messages.

I attempted to record more voices of ghosts from within the cemetery. Wanting to rule out coincidence, would I again hear more requests for help? I turned the ghost box on one more time that day.

"Help. Help me." There it was again, almost immediately.

"I appear to be recording help messages almost continually," I thought.

After a few more minutes I wanted to leave. "I'm gonna' walk back to my car. Is that alright?"

"Do not abandon," came out of the speaker right before I turned the device off.

I now felt even worse. There was no discounting what was happening. I kept hearing pleas for my help, but I wasn't able to answer the cries. I felt numb as I headed home. My first attempt at recording in a cemetery was both bitter and sweet. "Why would ghosts want to be found in graveyards when there are so many more appealing places?" I mumbled to myself.

The next day I thought about these events. My ghost box experiments had captivated me, taking me on an interesting journey. Were my experiences real, or had my mind simply been tricked into believing what I hoped would be true? More experiments were required. I wanted to return to *Massillon State Hospital* and *Massillon Cemetery* at night, but this time I would not go it alone. After all, I wanted someone of higher intelligence to accompany me in order to witness what I was hearing and experiencing. If I were becoming a bit delusional, such a person might be able to set me straight. I knew just the man for the task.

I am thankful to have all sorts of different friends I can call on to accompany me on whatever strange venture I deem necessary. My friend, Martin, was my logical choice, because I knew he wouldn't refuse the opportunity to do something so unusual. He was also rational and intelligent. I phoned him and set a time to pick him up, easily convincing him to walk the grounds with me of old *Massillon State* at night. Most people would refuse such an invitation. I think he was rather intrigued by the whole idea.

My plan was to return to the McKinley building west steps and record new ghost box sessions. I also wanted to pay another visit to the cemetery just down the road. Twelve days after my initial visit, Martin and I did just that. After arriving around ten in the evening, we walked from my car down a sidewalk and toward the buildings of *Massillon State Hospital*.

Martin and I first met by attending church together a decade earlier. We became good friends and had shared quite a few spiritual experiences with one another. So, it was not unusual when Martin turned to me halfway down that dark sidewalk and asked, "Do you feel that?"

"Yes." I knew instantly what Martin was asking me.

Goose bumps had dotted our skin at the same precise time as if we had walked into a cloud of invisible energy. We suddenly knew there was a presence with us. We were not alone. Was it a ghost that desired our attention or a spirit coming to help us in our endeavors? We did not know for sure, but something was happening and we welcomed its company.

The heavy presence accompanied us to the west steps and remained as we put the ghost box prototype into action. During this experience, both Martin and I felt like there were eyes upon us the entire time. Someone unseen was observing our activities, and we just knew it was not one but many.

As expected, the voices rang out from the ghost communicator but this time the messages were too many to count. They came through in bunches, much like people talking over one another. I remember switching the noisy instrument off to ask Martin what he heard. He described recognizing innumerable cries for help that broke the silence of the cool evening air. I was relieved to hear someone else also heard the same things as me. Both of us became very determined to attempt to help the hurting spirits. After some discussion, I suggested we speak to them much like a preacher might do before his congregation. What else could we do but follow our gut instinct? I began my message to the ghosts by declaring that their fears were false.

"Your fear has held you captive to the past and isolated you from family and friends," I shared, following whatever inspiration ushered forth from within me.

"You must let go of all fear, whatever it may be; choose to head to the light, should you see it. Do not fear, for family and friends are in the light. They are with you now, even. Reach out and take their hands."

As I spoke, I could see moving shadows from the corners of my eyes and heard the sound of shuffling feet just behind us. Was I reaching these ghosts? Martin also took his turn speaking to them, seeking to enlighten their pained minds with whatever truth would set them free. We instinctively worked together to attempt to lead the hurting spirits out of the false prison that their imagination must have created.

After Martin finished speaking, he asked me excitedly, "Did you see that?"

"See what?" I returned, very much intrigued.

"Over there, after we finished speaking, a mass of glowing light manifested then slowly dissipated as if many ghosts headed into the light and were rescued."

"Where did you see this?" I asked Martin. He walked over and stood close to the porch's red, brick wall.

"Right there," he pointed.

Just then, about five bricks glowed radiantly as if almost by command of Martin's finger. As I studied the phenomenon taking place before my eyes, I noticed the illumination of the bricks was very specific and not outside of the mortar that surrounded the five. I blinked my eyes a couple of times, because I couldn't believe what I was seeing. Then, I waved my hands over the bricks to see if I could block the glowing light if it originated from somewhere else. It was impossible. I had wondered about car headlights from the distance possibly shining upon the wall even though there was no incoming light. At that point, the glowing slowly receded and the bricks returned to red in front of us again. I had never witnessed such an anomaly.

"Did you see that?" I shockingly stammered.

"Uh yeah, but that wasn't what I had seen previously," Martin shot back matter-of-factly.

"Yeah, but did you *see* that?" I asked again, this time a bit aggravated.

"Yes, I did." Martin politely answered. I was glad he saw it, too.

"Amazing," was all I could utter, being completely blown away by the sight that we had both witnessed. I wished I could have also observed the glowing mass of light that preceded the luminous bricks. We questioned whether we had created the light we perceived the ghosts had headed into or if we simply opened their minds to its existence.

A few minutes later, we moved to an alcove on the other side of the brick structure and turned on the ghost box prototype in almost pitch black darkness. Something attracted us to this specific area outside of the McKinley building. As we listened to the ghost box audio, we began to feel uncomfortable in this location. We could hear someone coming through, but the messages were indistinguishable and, remarkably, without any pleas for help. I had thought that I had heard the name "Tom," but I was unsure. I would make certain to examine all of the recordings later after I had time to upload them to my computer.

It had been an hour of recording and speaking, so we moved our experiment to *Massillon Cemetery*. We were unable to gain access to the older section I had visited prior, but we noticed that a newer section across the street didn't have any gates. We drove back in until we were surrounded by tombstones. I gravitated to a spot near the middle and listened to the ghost box as it swept the FM band.

"Help. Help. Help me. Help!" immediately came forth.

There were many desperate voices similar to what we had heard while at *Massillon State Hospital*. Like before, I took the time to speak aloud to those whom I knew were listening but could not see with my eyes.

Afterward, a new idea had come to me. "Let's turn on the ghost communicator and see if the help messages have gone away. If we truly assisted ghosts, then there should be a noticeable difference in the communications," I told Martin. He agreed. I flipped on the switch to the ghost box. The audio noise had changed. We did not hear the constant pleading for help that we had heard prior.

I decided to ask a question directed to any enlightened spirits that may have been listening to us.

"Have they headed to the light?"

"The light, yeah," was the reply that was heard by both of us.

"Did that help a lot of earthbound spirits?" I further questioned.

We thought we heard, "Yeah, it did."

We left after that and headed home. It was difficult to sleep after the evening's excitement, especially knowing we had probably collected some great audio that might reveal more about what had occurred that evening.

My mind raced as I lay in bed retracing the events from that night. The answers we received seemed to confirm my suspicions that enlightened spirits often attempt to help ghosts. To me, what we had experienced could be likened to the resurrection of the dead that I had read about in the Bible. Although our experience differed from the idea of a physical resurrection that I had been taught in church, I could not shake the thought from my mind. Accounts of resurrection found within biblical texts appear to be allegories that point to something greater than just a literal interpretation. What hidden meaning might they hold? Could it be that human spirits sometimes suffer in a hell of their own creation, but we are able to help resurrect them from death to life? I was feeling that resurrection was about people breaking free from their fears formed in the past in order to finally receive love and forgiveness in the present.

The next day, I was excited to analyze the audio files I had recorded with Martin at *Massillon State Hospital* and *Massillon Cemetery*. Would the recordings support what we thought we had heard live while on-site. The audio files from the McKinley building's west porch captured an echo effect due to the cave-like nature of its design. Still, there were many interesting messages captured by my recorder. I had to laugh because some of the words were profane. Someone had called me a foul name and told me off in the beginning of the session. After that, confirmation of the help messages we had heard was found in the recordings.

"Help me. Help me to...the light."

"Are you in pain?" I had asked after hearing multiple requests for help.

"Pain"

I heard more interesting words come through my headset.

"Help. Spirit."

"Don't quit."

"Want help."

These messages only further confirmed our findings from that evening. The little alcove on the other side of the building, where we had felt uncomfortable, also provided an interesting message or two.

"Spirit of Tom," rang through the ghost box communicator and prompted a discussion between Martin and me.

"Spirit of somebody...spirit of whom?" I asked.

"Tom," was heard in response again.

Then, I couldn't believe my ears. It was as if a discussion was ensuing between two earthbound spirits about Martin and me!

"(I'm) coming through this thing." I took this to mean the ghost box, as if the ghost was shocked he could be heard through the speaker.

"Does he look bad?" This response sounded like an unseen ghost was afraid of us.

Unfortunately, I had turned the ghost box off shortly after that and we left the alcove, being oblivious to a final message that I recorded while there.

"Help us. Wait. Help."

It was after this encounter in the alcove that we left to visit the nearby *Massillon Cemetery*. When I listened to the recording made at the center of the burial site from when we had first arrived, there were many requests for help just like we had witnessed firsthand. There must have been quite a few disorderly, disembodied spirits attempting to communicate at once, making it nearly impossible to detect more than one or two words within each phrase. The voices were a jumbled mess due to them talking over one another.

I became intrigued by the recording I made from when I had spoken to the lost spirits in the cemetery yard. As I mentioned prior, we both had heard confirmation of the ghosts having headed to the light, and the audio fully supported our experience.

"Did that help a lot of earthbound spirits?" my voice inquired from the enlightened spirit who had confirmed our work.

"Yeah, it did." The response was on the recording just as we thought we had heard while in the cemetery.

After this exchange, there was one more plea for help that came through the ghost communicator that I had not mentioned. This voice sounded female and also desired to head to the light. Martin and I had worked to help her cross over using the ghost box to answer her questions. I had sensed that my grandmother, Audrey, was there to help me; and so, I asked her to help the female ghost. The following exchange was recorded from that evening in the cemetery.

"Does she see you Grandma Audrey?" I asked.

"My spirit," came through the ghost box.

"If you can, I want you to go with my Grandma Audrey and trust her to take you to the light. Can you do that?" I asked the lost, female spirit.

"Thanks. Goodbye," was the polite response.

I had to get confirmation. "Does she still need help or has she moved on?" I questioned.

"Through."

"Did she go *through* to the light?" I wondered aloud.

"Yeah."

The communications we captured that night in Massillon further confirmed what I had been concluding about ghost rescue. It compelled me to experiment further to learn about ghost behavior. My ideas about helping ghosts were consistently being affirmed by actual experiences and evidence.

I soon had another opportunity to test the ghost box prototype, and this time it was at a famous haunted site. While vacationing with my family in Florida, I scheduled a visit to the *St. Augustine Lighthouse*. Having scheduled a time that I could climb the lighthouse tower alone, we made our way north toward St. Augustine from Orlando.

The *St. Augustine Lighthouse* has a long history of ghost

sightings. Both adults and children have been seen and heard on the grounds. The original lighthouse was first built by Spanish settlers in the 1600s. In 1824, it became an official United States lighthouse in one of the oldest cities in North America, St. Augustine. The current light tower replaced its predecessor in 1874, as the original had been lost to erosion.

The history of the lighthouse haunting may very well originate with Mr. Andreu, a lighthouse keeper who tragically fell to his death while painting the original tower. However, some believe the haunting might stem back to land disputes among neighbors who sold their parcels to the U.S. Government for the current light; several tour guides have reportedly seen one of the original land owners, Dr. Ballard, walking the grounds.

Still, the worst tragedy to have befallen the lighthouse was the death of Hezekiah Pittee's daughters and their playmate. All three drowned while playing in a handcart used to carry supplies from ships. It accidentally fell off its tramway into the ocean, carrying all three girls to their deaths. Ghosts of children have been spotted at the *St. Augustine Lighthouse*, but no one knows for sure if any of the sightings were of the three young ladies.

St. Augustine Lighthouse is also home to other paranormal phenomena typical to a haunting, such as footsteps, the smells of cigar smoke, moving shadows, and disembodied voices. I wanted to attempt to capture some of the latter, so I climbed the metal spiral stairs of the tower and made my way to the top of the empty lighthouse by myself.

Within the recordings I made inside the lighthouse tower, I heard the voices of both children and adults coming through the ghost box. Similar to my experience at *Massillon State Hospital*, I heard ghosts discussing me in the audio right after I first turned it on.

"Who is he?" rang out as I listened intently to the speaker and its sound.

After hearing what I thought were several help messages, I then heard someone distinctly say, "Help us to see." This voice came through the ghost box very clearly.

"Talk with her."

"Talk with who?" I wondered to myself. So, I asked, "Who needs help?"

"The keeper." This reply was very relevant, especially because it was recorded in a lighthouse.

As I asked questions, I worked my way back down the narrow, circular stairway. I wanted to stay and help, but I was doing this around the time the museum closed. I needed to get back down so they could lock the tower up for the night.

"I'm gonna' lock the tower, is that good?" I asked, nearing the bottom of the lighthouse.

"Light on. Leave it off." I was stunned by this request.

I gathered my wits and said, "Good night."

"G' night." I had heard the word "night" quite clearly as it echoed inside the tower.

I learned quite a bit from my trip to St. Augustine, having tested this form of ghost communication in another part of the country. The ghost box prototype worked well even though I was 900 miles away from home. Most important, this trip confirmed for me that there are ghosts everywhere who need our help. This experiment helped me to continue formulating my method for helping lost spirits find the light. I just needed to practice my ideas more out in the field.

Another *SIGHT* Mystery Night presented itself as an opportunity to test my theories further, so I decided to attend the gathering at the *Old Town Hall* that sits on the square in Tallmadge, Ohio. Known locally for reports of ghosts that supposedly haunt the building, I thought this might be an interesting place to conduct more ghost box experiments. Although I recorded several messages inside the *Old Town Hall*, it did not seem that they came from ghosts haunting the historical building. Maybe, the voices were just spirits who were with me. I wasn't sure. As I stood upon the upstairs landing of the old building, I found myself looking out across the property to the church that sits behind the *Old Town Hall.* I was then compelled to ask questions about it.

"Do you see the church?" I queried.

"Old Church" was the reply through the ghost box prototype.

Not long after, I decided to leave the *Old Town Hall* and cross the grass lawn to the steps of the old church that sits on the other side of the *Tallmadge Town Square*. I instantly felt a spirit presence when I got there, much like I had felt at *Massillon State Hospital.* My skin was electrified with goose bumps once again. As if on cue, "help messages" began pouring forth from the ghost box. This had not happened when I used the device in the *Old Town Hall*. Two *SIGHT* members, who had joined me, immediately heard "help" or "help me" emanating from the noisy communicator. I decided to ask a question or two.

"Do spirits need help?"

"In trouble," was the reply.

"So, do you need help?" I questioned further.

"Help. People passed don't know it," came through the speaker. This message was hurried and almost rhythmic. Often, ghost box EVP will follow the rhythmic pattern caused by the sweeping radio's changing frequencies. Sometimes, when I record my voice while the ghost box is running, it will also sound rhythmic, staccato-like.

After hearing the help messages at the church in Tallmadge, several members within *SIGHT* wanted to focus our efforts upon helping ghosts cross to the light. I was thankful for the assistance. Like me, they also desired to become better at communicating with earthbound spirits. Our hope was to help ghosts overcome the issues that imprisoned them. I do not recall exactly what we shared with the ghosts who were listening to our words that night in Tallmadge, but I know we worked together to alleviate their fears. The hurting souls no longer begged for our attention; we had helped them and were rewarded with what I now call the "release." When ghosts leave the past behind and head unto the light, I noticed there is a release of tangible, spirit presence. I would describe it as a feeling of intense joy and peace. This cleansing energy is a blessing that we can experience. It is a real confirmation of the success of ghost rescue work.

SIGHT continued investigating paranormal disturbances within residences, businesses and historical sites. Using the combination of both technical and psychic teams, the group worked together to solve claims of haunting within northeast Ohio. As we ventured from case to case, I was becoming particularly interested in finding more fearful examples of haunting to investigate.

Fear was not something that would easily dissuade me, for my mind was strong to the task. In order to learn, we needed to move beyond beliefs and face our fears, working to overcome them through knowledge. I knew remaining fearless would be crucial to not only calming troubled home owners but paramount in order to reach lost souls who were trapped by fear itself. Unlike most ghost investigators, I no longer felt the need to prove the existence of ghosts. I knew ghosts existed. Now, I wanted to know how we could help them and if it would be possible to free every hurting soul.

Chapter Five

Investigations of the Haunted

As SIGHT evolved over time, the ghost investigation group came to agree that its mission wasn't solely to prove the existence of ghosts but to work to learn how we could help them. Still, it was important to gather evidence of ghosts in order to further discern what might be happening with each case of haunting we embraced.

The group had members who preferred to operate electronics during ghost investigations, utilizing devices such as camcorders, digital cameras, audio recorders, thermometers, and EMF meters. *SIGHT* also benefited by having members gifted with intuitive abilities. I found myself doing a little of both. I enjoyed experimenting with the ghost box prototype and recording EVP in conjunction with following my inner leading. As a group we felt it was also important to pay attention to the stories surrounding the haunting and take detailed notes. Eyewitness accounts can provide direction for an investigation and be used to corroborate any technical and psychic evidences we might later collect. This method gave us three sources from which to gather evidence. Then, we could piece together a story that helped us to determine what we needed to do to benefit both the haunted and the haunter.

While each investigation unfolded, we were able to gain an understanding of what was occurring. Our work would quickly turn toward ghost communication once we had direction. We worked on the premise that if we could speak with the unquiet dead, we might be able to ease their suffering. After all, ghosts are hurting people who have been silenced. I was finding that they often look for an ear to hear what they have to say.

As we worked on listening and communicating, our intention was to help resolve any issues that may have created a roadblock to the person in spirit. Sometimes, solving ghosts' problems came down to more than just resolving "unfinished business" as some investigators like to call it. Quite often, we felt like Sherlock Holmes piecing together bits of information, sometimes becoming discouraged if the trail fell cold. Still, with persistence and patience it was possible to get to the object of most ghosts' concerns.

Communicating with suffering people, especially those who are obstinate or even mean, can be difficult at times. Ghosts are no different than us in that respect. We learned this through experience. Surprisingly, not every ghost wants our help. Some worked against us in every way possible, even if it resulted in hiding or isolation. To say that all ghosts have "unfinished business" that needs resolved seems too tidy a conclusion after examining the ghost condition. Not every person who dies leaves behind a bucket list of unfinished tasks that need resolved. Ghosts can remain earthbound for many other reasons. Some specters do not know what they want and seem content to remain that way.

As I worked with the ghost box during investigations with *SIGHT*, I continued to receive help messages. Once this began, it never changed. I mentioned that it was as if news spread in the spirit world that I could hear their words. The consistency of these messages helped me to understand the condition of those who begged for my attention.

In a sense, the breadth of humanity was revealed through the voices and messages I recorded with *SIGHT*. I learned that ghosts come in all sorts of packages. Some ghosts appeared to be feminine, while others were male. Ghosts may be young, old, loud, or soft-spoken. Many seemed very loving, caring, and sometimes funny, while other ghosts were dry-witted, grumpy, or even domineering. Yet as people, they were and are fascinating studies in human behavior to me. The work only confirmed for us that ghosts are real, hurting people who often cry out for anyone to hear them. Many times, we found that giving them an ear was all it took to release them from their pain.

Through the aid of the ghost box I mentioned I was fortunate enough to occasionally record disembodied voices discussing me or others present with me. I also noted that the device appeared to act as a carrier of sound waves that somehow amplified ghost and spirit voices. Its effects seemed to occur whether the ghosts wanted it to or not. It appeared I had found a great tool to eavesdrop on ghosts and hear what they were thinking. The more I used the ghost box, the better and more consistent these communications became. I also learned to improve my listening skills.

During our attempts to speak with ghosts, enlightened spirits also would come through the ghost box to converse with us. We were often aware of their unseen work to help ghosts find the light. A true tag-team effort could be detected taking place during spirit rescues; the intuitive people within *SIGHT* also picked up on this. We noticed that while we were helping ghosts transition to the light, quite often other ghosts would join them so as to not miss the opportunity to go home. How did they know to find us in order to be helped? Did enlightened spirits bring them to us for aid, or were some ghosts attracted to the presence of the light that we created through the power of our intentions? It is, of course, possible that maybe more ghosts walk among us than we might imagine. If so, could they listen in on our conversations and simply follow us to take part in whatever they like? I suggest it's possible.

The first *SIGHT* case of note that proved the worth of the ghost box was the investigation of an older, two-story home in a small, quaint town. When the *SIGHT* team arrived during the day, the lady of the house, Wendy, proceeded to tell us about hearing strange noises upstairs, especially talking. Apparently, the voice seemed to resonate through the vents in the bedroom. She also noticed, from time to time, that personal items would go missing. She would later find them back in their proper place where she had already searched!

It was within the master bedroom that Wendy also experienced a weighty presence pressing down on her one night while lying in bed. That ghastly event, coupled with footsteps being heard traveling up and down the steps by several family members, caused her to become alarmed. Desperate for help, she secretly had us visit her home while her husband was away at work.

After listening to Wendy's account of phantom activity, I enjoyed attempting to piece together a picture of what may have been causing the disturbance within her residence. I always try to make note of the details, asking good questions so that I can formulate a theory to work with. Why would the ghost of a human behave oddly by hiding things, making vocal sounds, and touching someone while asleep? I am often left with the conclusion that strange behavior is likely the result of a desperate person willing to try anything to gain another's attention.

I desired to ask Wendy a few questions to get to the bottom of things. Being a very new member of *SIGHT*, I felt it best to first request permission from the group to do so. They welcomed my input and allowed me to ask some questions.

"Has someone recently passed that was either a friend or family member?"

"No. Not really. My father-in-law, Ted, died about 16 years ago, though," she responded.

"Was he close to the family?"

"Yes, he was. Ted was very close to my husband. He was his favorite son," Wendy told us.

"Did anything unusual happen after your father-in-law died?" My question made her pause for a moment.

"Now that I think of it, right after his funeral is when we first noticed the footsteps and some missing items. Ted was a hard-headed man with little respect for women," she informed us.

I felt completely drawn to the fact that some of the activity in the house had begun right after Ted's funeral. Was he trying to get their attention to let them know he was alright? We explored the home as a team to attempt to collect physical evidence and gather some psychic impressions. All of us, including our psychic-mediums, struggled to piece together what might be happening. For some unknown reason, the ghost seemed to be hiding. This was unusual, but we've learned through experience to keep pushing forward until something breaks during an investigation.

Several of us decided to use the ghost box prototype to see if any answers could be received. As we turned it on and listened, we didn't hear messages coming through it. It was very frustrating. We asked questions, but it did not seem like we were able to get any responses that we could describe as intelligent.

"What was going on here?" I wondered.

Although we had not detected anything in the home intuitively or with any of the ghost detection equipment, I perceived that Ted desired our help. I was not certain of this, but the thought of him remained continually on my heart. I sort of ignored this nagging inside me until we had no other direction from which to work. My questioning became very pointed when I turned on the ghost box for a second time.

"What can you tell me about the father-in-law? Is he still here?" I asked. "Does Ted need help?"

Nothing seemed to come through the ghost communicator so I turned it off, remaining frustrated. As the investigation continued, the thought of Ted would not leave me. I knew we needed to help this man, but I needed proof. Quietly, I slipped downstairs to the front foyer and covertly listened to the audio recording I had just made using a pair of headphones.

I struggled to hear any messages on the recording, similar to what we collectively witnessed upstairs during the live ghost box session. The chatter in the audio was garbled and noisy. Then, I heard an unbelievable message within the audio recording. It followed my questioning about Ted.

"He never...crossed!" burst through the headset and stunned me. I replayed the audio once more.

"He never...crossed!" I heard it again, clear as day.

I frequently describe the rescue of ghosts as helping them to cross over to the light. The message confirmed what I had known within my heart about Ted: He had never crossed over to the light. It was an intelligent, direct response to my question. Excited, I gathered some of the team together and played it for them. They also heard it clearly.

We then played the message for the homeowner as we explained that sometimes people remain behind and do not go to the light. I shared with Wendy my suspicions that perhaps her father-in-law had been trying make her husband aware of his presence without success. Maybe it took Ted a decade to become better at his attempts to break through the veil to communicate with the family. I suspected that Ted had decided to switch gears and see if he could grab Wendy's attention instead. Wendy confirmed that her husband was not open to the idea of ghosts or spirit communication and likely would be closed-minded to such attempts by his own father. In fact, his closed-mindedness is why she had us visit the home while he was away at work. She felt that Ted would have preferred to speak with a man, so her husband would have been his logical first choice. Maybe my theory had been correct.

After explaining to Wendy that we wanted to help her father-in-law find his way to the light, she consented. A few of us gathered in an upstairs bedroom where the audio recording had been made and proceeded to speak. After a while, I just shared my heart openly with Ted. I instructed him of his condition and that the light was where he needed to go to continue living his life, leaving the past behind. By mentally imagining the light, we easily allowed Ted to slip away but not before he gave a parting message to Laura Lyn psychically.

"Thank you, Louis."

During Ted's crossing, I felt a rush of energy flow through my body several times. It was a confirmation of his crossing; the release of loving waves of joy and peace made me feel whole. Such a healing witness to this work is something to be relished and a reward all its own.

The *SIGHT* ghost investigations allowed me to test and prove my theories over and over again. Each circumstance presented a unique opportunity to understand more about why ghosts haunt and what can be done to assist them. There simply was not one blanket explanation that could explain the reason behind every haunting we encountered. Each situation was unfortunately different. I had really hoped to find one common theme woven within the ghost psyche.

I was determined to plow ahead, remaining unafraid in my work. One case, in particular, intrigued me. Patty and Bill lived out in the country in a small rural community. They had moved Patty's father into an upstairs bedroom of their old, two-story home. He was getting up in years and required their loving care. Patty had contacted *SIGHT* about some strange activity involving her father and their home.

Arriving at their house first, I was welcomed by two gracious hosts in a home filled with antiques and heirlooms. I relaxed in a chair in their living room and began listening to their stories of what sounded like a very active, female ghost.

Bill and Patty had both experienced objects moving in their home. They also had their house alarm go off frequently and heard strange noises in the basement. Both Patty and Bill had witnessed shadows moving about the living room. My ears perked up when they mentioned moving shadows, because some of the other phenomena could have been caused by natural occurrences instead of ghosts. Patty then urged Bill to tell me what he had seen in the home. Bill described seeing an apparition of an older woman. She appeared before him for maybe three to five seconds, enough time for him to get a good look at her. He believed she was Betty, the heavy-set, former owner of the house.

Betty had lived in this home for about 40 years and then passed away in it. Her son had inherited the property, renting the house to Patty and Bill. They told me what disturbed them most was hearing Patty's father occasionally talking with someone upstairs. When questioned about whom he was talking to, the 86 year-old man replied, "The lady who hides in my closet!"

We were then interrupted by more *SIGHT* members who had finally arrived at the home. The house was a bit difficult to spot in the dark, so they had some difficulty finding it. As soon as she entered the door, psychic-medium Laura Lyn wanted to walk through the house, preferring to remain unaware of any details about the haunting. I made sure we did not tell her about Betty.

During her walk through the kitchen area, she intuitively heard the name "Elizabeth." I stopped everyone, informing them she was correct in what she had discerned. The name Betty is often a nickname for Elizabeth. We worked our way through the house exploring the downstairs first, and then made our way upstairs. As we entered the master bedroom, we could feel an intense spirit presence come upon us. The invisible energy caused goose bumps to appear on my arms and neck. We were quite certain the presence of the older woman Bill had described was now with us.

I had brought several ghost box models to experiment with that night. Turning our attention to the crackling audio, we listened intently with anticipation. Betty seemed quite adept at manipulating objects and interacting with people in the home, so it seemed only natural that we should expect to hear a message from her.

We heard a "help" come through the first ghost box I switched on. I would later find that I had also recorded the name "Betty." The second ghost box session yielded a few more messages, perhaps because our intentions were made clearer. We wanted to communicate with Betty and help her.

"Help. Help us. Help Betty," reverberated through the device.

"Are you a ghost or are you a spirit, Betty?" I asked. I was trying to figure out who was speaking with us.

"Spirit. Help." This answer seemed odd to me, but I also knew that whoever answered might not share my same definitions for the words "ghost" and "spirit."

"Why are you here?" someone in our group questioned.

"Her son," was the rapid response. Now we were getting somewhere. It sounded like someone else in spirit was speaking on Betty's behalf.

"Is it because of your son, Betty?" I jumped in and questioned.

"Yes, to help her son," came through the audio, though musically as if it were sung.

Just then, we had an interruption. Psychic-medium Laura Lyn chimed in that there was a young girl's presence with us, and she was demanding our attention.

"Did someone say, 'Help me'?" Laura Lyn took over the questioning.

"Help me," came through the ghost box distinctly and in a young child's voice.

"What's your name?" Laura Lyn asked.

"Cara." The voice again sounded childlike, maybe seven years old. Laura Lyn asked the group if we heard the name Cara come through the ghost box. Of course, we did.

"Are you looking for somebody?" Laura Lyn asked, following her intuition.

"Help me to find them." The response was slow and heartbreaking.

We felt she was looking to reunite with her family. Turning the ghost box off, we worked to help the young girl to the light and with loved ones in spirit. She moved forward quite easily. Whether she was somehow trapped in the house or brought to us for help, I cannot be certain. Later, as I reviewed my recordings from that night, her desperate responses to Laura Lyn's questions could be heard in my headphones. The little girl ghost was there just as we had thought.

We still had a job to do with Betty. At this point, we knew she needed help getting to the light but did not want to go due to her son. Betty was earthbound and not in a state of peace. Many times when helping lost spirits, Laura Lyn will act as a medium so the ghost can speak through her vocal chords. When this occurs, it is possible for different members of our group to converse directly with the ghost. Mediumship can make the job of helping ghosts much easier.

As we worked further to attempt to understand why Betty remained behind in her former residence, the story began to emerge. This haunting turned out to be a classic case of unfinished business. Betty had a message for her son: Don't sell the house. We later learned that her son had been toying with the idea of selling the property, even though he suspected his mother had remained behind in the home after her death. Betty was truly attached to the place and didn't share her son's desire to part with it. It was her wish for the house to remain in the family. She wanted it to eventually pass down to her grandchildren. By remaining behind, she also wanted to be near her family and watch over their lives. Once we understood this, we were able to promise her we would convey the message to Bill and Patty; they would in turn pass it on to her son. After convincing Betty that she needed to move forward in life by heading into the light, she elected to cross most willingly. We had to assure her that she could return and visit loved ones after she left. Not only did Betty find comfort knowing that her last wishes would reach her son, but both Patty and Bill were also able to have closure.

Probably the biggest confirmation of our success with helping ghosts has been the response of the families whom we've worked with. It's been said that "no news is good news," and this often holds true with ghost investigation. If you solve the issue correctly, the haunting should subside. I like to hear follow-up reports from formerly distressed families whom we have helped, especially when they no longer require our assistance. Of course, it is just as rewarding to know we have helped people who are invisible to us in spirit.

As I explored more ghosts and haunting through investigations with *SIGHT*, I desired strongly to attempt to work with disembodied spirits that displayed even greater negative behavior. If we truly wanted to learn how to help lost spirits, we couldn't be afraid to encounter the worst of cases. When we did eventually encounter such earthbound spirits, I was of the mindset that nothing seen or unseen was going to intimidate me.

Working with problem ghosts requires patience. Take note. Lewd behavior exhibited by foul-minded spirits may anger even the calmest ghost investigator, especially if children have been the victim of a haunting. Try and remain cool-headed when communicating with ghosts. At times, arrogance on my part did not help; I caught myself becoming agitated to the point of badgering headstrong spirits. This would almost always create a breakdown in communication while a battle of egos ensued between me and the ghost. When this occurred, the group could actually feel the tension in the atmosphere. Eventually, I realized that ghosts were not an opposing enemy we must fight but defensive, wounded people who require our compassion. Like with any human relationship, I needed to learn to love, not attack, those who frustrated me; otherwise, it would be impossible to have a productive conversation. It can be a difficult lesson to learn.

This brings a certain investigation to mind. It involved a ghost that plagued a small child and mother. The mother, Amy, told us that both she and her daughter had seen a shadowy man in their home that would touch them, watch them, and make noises late at night. The three-year-old child described the entity as the "man with red eyes" and consequently was afraid to sleep in her bedroom. Who could blame her?

Most of the disturbances seemed to be located in the hallway and bedrooms, though they reported hearing noises in the attic. The outside of the house was populated with small, wild animals, and my check of the attic confirmed my suspicions that rodents had been responsible for some of the noises heard at night. Still, mice didn't explain the moving shadow seen by two of the home's residents.

When we investigated the house, the bedrooms indeed drew our attention. I strongly felt there was a man hiding in the closet of the little girl's room. I knew he had been making himself appear scary to those who could see him. I suspected the red eyes and frightening face was just a trick used by the ghost to frighten Amy and her daughter.

The rest of the team joined me in the small bedroom. We decided to open the bifold doors of the closet, letting the hidden man know we were aware of his presence. Psychic-medium Laura Lyn saw him at once, but she described his appearance as being devilish-looking with skull and horns. We chose not to believe that was his real image, and I told him so. I don't believe in demons, so such a trick couldn't work on me. After all, he was seen with red eyes by the little girl, so I deduced he was very capable of enhancing his appearance for his benefit.

Laura Lyn had perceived that the man had been in the home for about nine years and wanted to remain there. Being able to manipulate people through fear, she told us he was quite content to amuse himself at the expense of others. This caused me to become angry with him, and I let him know he was a coward. He became unwilling to talk with me after that, and I needed to cool off. I struggled to do so.

My frustration with this ghost led to an unproductive ghost box session in the same room.

"Are there people in here with us?" I asked, wondering if there were any other ghosts in the home.

"I am," was the response from the man in the closet, now using the ghost box to speak with us.

"How long have you been here?" Laura Lyn asked.

"Stay here."

"(You) stay here?" Laura Lyn responded.

"Oh, it's fun," the group heard together through the device, my blood now boiling. I kept thinking of the poor little girl and the thought of this man causing her to be afraid in her own bedroom.

"Is it true you've been here nine years?" I demanded.

"Impossible," shot back the man. I figured he must have lost track of time.

This man was lost. Laura Lyn told us that he didn't want to talk with me any longer. It was then that I calmed down, drew a deep breath, and thought about the situation. If I were to help this man and the family who lived here, I needed to deliver an impassioned plea to make him listen. With my disgust put aside, I must have spoken for about ten minutes. I knew the man understood he was a ghost and that he was aware of the light. Yet, I needed find the source of his pain in order to make him desire to change his situation. Knowing that reuniting the man with loved ones who had already crossed to the light might work, I decided to take that approach in my communication. When we draw upon our fondest memories, those recollections can evoke powerful emotions that almost transport us back in time. This man needed to begin thinking about those who knew and loved him.

With the help of Laura Lyn's mediumistic abilities, we were able to talk with the man about his mother. After we took the time to help him work through his fear of having disappointed her, he willingly moved into the light to be with his mom once again. The man had once used fear to haunt and manipulate others. Now, he chose to face his own fears that had haunted him. It was exhilarating to feel his cleansing release fill the atmosphere of the room as he made his journey home. All was forgiven.

Perhaps one of the saddest and most difficult cases of haunting I worked on with *SIGHT* took place in a small apartment in Canton, Ohio. Figuring out the situation and resolving it took several visits utilizing different skilled team members. Eventually, *SIGHT* was successful in solving what had become a very puzzling situation. To this day it remains one of the most memorable of investigations. Occasionally, I still hear reports of the family being completely at peace now.

I shared that ghosts can cry out for our help and do odd things to gain our attention. This might not always be the case; but when extreme paranormal activity takes place within a home, it usually is because a ghost has become desperate to be heard. Tricia's haunting was an example of extreme desperation.

A week before her father died, Tricia's family had noticed some odd things beginning to occur at their small apartment. Lou had been on life support but was eventually pronounced dead after falling down a flight of stairs while drunk at his parent's house. This tragic accident happened just down the street from the apartment. His daughter, Tricia, was 12 years old and lived with his ex-wife Laura and their 14 year old son, Lou Jr., and their seven year old daughter, Millie. Laura also had a four year old daughter who lived with them from another relationship. Tricia captured her daddy's heart, and he often called her "Princess." All three children meant the world to him, though.

The family began noticing an odd feeling around them, especially near Tricia. Light fixtures continually blowing bulbs and phantom telephone calls with no one on the other end of the phone line, left them confused. When the youngest child saw a pale man with boots, a green hat, and brown hair in Laura's bedroom, the family became horrified. The little girl knew the man, saying he was "Milly's daddy." Lou was haunting their apartment.

Having lived in the apartment for only six months, Laura had moved there with her children in the midst of a nasty divorce. The activity began on February 11th and took place for a solid month before *SIGHT* was asked to come and investigate. The family was tired of hearing strange bangs, seeing weird lights moving in and out of Laura's bedroom, and finding items related to Lou being knocked off shelves.

They knew they were being haunted by Laura's ex-husband but didn't know the reason behind the perceived attack. The divorce had caused hurt feelings between Laura and Lou to the point a civil protection order had been requested. Laura thought maybe Lou wanted some payback for the anguish the separation had caused him. Her theory about the haunting sounded quite plausible to me.

After we interviewed Laura, she showed us around the apartment, leading us into the basement. Medium Laura Lyn and another psychic of Native American descent, Ben, detected a strong, negative, male energy residing in one corner. They sensed he had lived in the apartment building prior to Laura moving in. We decided to leave him alone, so we could try and find Lou. The psychics did not come in contact with Lou while downstairs but eventually sensed him after we made our way upstairs to Tricia's bedroom. Her room soon became central to our ghost investigation.

SIGHT had requested prior that all children be removed from the home while we investigated. This allowed us to have more room to move about and not be interrupted. As I walked around the apartment, I and the others were drawn to Tricia's bedroom. We elected to record the ghost box prototype in the small bedroom and see if we could communicate with Lou. I turned the device on with three of us in the room.

"I want to know if Lou is here tonight," I declared openly to the room with my audio recorder operating.

"Lou...Lou. Lou," was heard by us in the skipping audio noise.

"Can you say 'Lou' again?" I asked, desiring a bit more confirmation.

"Listen...Lou," we heard.

"Lou, I'm hearing you. Can you please say 'Lou' again?"

"Lou."

"Do you understand I'm here to help you?" I asked. I was now convinced we were communicating with the ghost.

"I do."

I wanted to make sure Lou understood that going to the light was something he shouldn't fear. I decided to inquire about his condition from enlightened spirits who I thought were there with us to help him.

"Spirit guides, does he understand this (heading to the light)?"

"He would. Help him to the light," was the response we recorded.

"Lou, you can come back here and visit your daughter still. Do you understand that?"

"Yes."

"Did you want to say you're sorry out loud (to Laura)?"

"Too sorry..."

"Do you have a message you would like delivered to Tricia and the other children?" I asked, feeling I was making some headway now.

"They may be able to help me." This didn't make sense to me. How could they help?

"Is there anything you'd like to say to Laura?" I wanted to help Lou clear his conscience.

"Spirit around Trish," was the odd response. "Help. Help. Help."

We ended the ghost communication session and attempted to help Lou cross over to the light by way of a spirit circle. A "spirit circle" is the term *SIGHT* uses for when the group gathers in a circle to intuitively communicate with earthbound spirits. This is how we collectively focus in order to help them find the light. We typically do not leave the circle until we feel the mission is complete and the ghost has crossed over. Following our perceptions, we worked together to speak to Lou while focusing our intention upon producing the light and guiding him into it. We struggled to get him to cross and remained unsure of our success.

After taking a short break to discuss what we had experienced, all of us agreed that we needed to do another ghost box session to see if Lou had made his way home. Gathering the entire *SIGHT* group into the small bedroom once again, I began encountering issues with the ghost box prototype. Operating erratically, it quit sweeping and landed on a radio station playing rock music. Then, it began sweeping again, though sounding very odd. After a few minutes of this, I turned it off after asking only a few questions. I thought the device was broken. At the time I hadn't realized that a ghost had manipulated the electronics of the device due to being unhappy with our presence and the ghost communicator.

The next morning, I slipped on my old pair of headphones and listened to all of the recordings I had made the previous evening at Laura's apartment. The second session of recordings seemed extremely weird, a real first for me.

"Please, son of a bitch, leave!" The ghost box message startled me as it somehow came out of manipulated music. The musical instruments of a song were twisted into the cryptic phrase. This was definitely not a song one might hear played on the radio, and I was unaware of it happening at the time.

"Did Lou cross?" my voice asked on the recording.

"He's back," came a reply from the spirit realm.

"How could Lou have come back," I thought to myself. This didn't make any sense to me.

Then, I heard my voice on the recording ask, "How am I getting a rock station?" This was during the investigation when the ghost box had stopped working and remained stuck on a local music station.

"Stop that music!" That was the second angry response from a disembodied spirit. The words were formed within the melody of an unrecognizable song. It was quite fantastic to hear. Someone at Laura's apartment was very upset at me after the ghost box had played some rock music for a few seconds. This ghost couldn't be Lou.

After I listened to the recordings again, I realized that Lou had not left. Even worse, we had not addressed a very angry ghost that also inhabited Laura's apartment. I was sure of this, because Lou had not acted mean to me or anyone else in the apartment before the second ghost box session. He had seemed glad to be communicating with us, but why did he choose not to leave?

I shared my concerns with others from *SIGHT* and it was not long before one of the members received a call from Laura. The family sensed that Lou was still there with them. The paranormal activity also seemed to be increasing. They witnessed more light bulbs popping in lamps, as well as their TV turning itself on and off. I now realized that these electrical disturbances could indeed be caused by a ghost, especially after the ghost communicator had behaved so strangely in the apartment. The abnormal events made the family even more frightened than before, so *SIGHT* dispatched another team to the apartment to try and settle the issue once and for all.

During the return visit, Laura Lyn and psychic Ben were able to confirm my suspicions of a different male spirit remaining attached to the apartment. Of course, they had detected this during the first investigation, but somehow we had overlooked it. They perceived that the male ghost was a former tenant who had died tragically. They also could tell that this angry individual was not in a good frame of mind and apparently had been attracted to Lou's daughter, Tricia. Lou had remained behind to protect her and the rest of his family from this man. Our attempts to get the negative ghost to leave were eventually successful. Somehow, the man was coaxed out of the apartment by Ben but not before following him home and attacking him while in his car. Ben had scratches that appeared on his body to prove it. Although most ghosts are not this ill-willed, it should be noted that some are quite capable of scratching or pushing people who aggravate them.

The haunting of Laura's apartment provided us an opportunity to make a wealth of observations, perhaps the most important being that desperate ghosts are capable of using everything at their disposal to gain people's attention. Secondly, the mental condition of ghosts, as well as the reasons they remain behind, can vary drastically from one soul to another. The complexity of the human mind is quite fascinating. We think and feel differently from one another, and it's the same with ghosts. There is simply not one broad-brush answer or method that will suffice as the solution to every haunting a person may encounter.

Although hurting people in spirit may choose to act negatively, as we witnessed in Laura's apartment, some can exhibit quite awful behavior. I have found that much of our interpretation of that behavior is often based upon our societal or religious beliefs. In Western cultures, anything dark and negative may have the tendency to be labeled as a "demon" due to strong Christian beliefs in a devil and his minions wreaking havoc upon the unsuspecting. Christianity created its teachings about demons for a purpose. It is well known that St. Augustine, St. Thomas Aquinas, and other early Christian leaders began forming these doctrines at least 300 years after the time of Jesus in order to control people through fear. Knowing the truth about the origin of demons allowed me to approach the negative entities we encountered as simply cases of mistaken identity. In other words, it is my view that negative spirits are not demons but simply lost people behaving poorly. We cannot help ill-mannered human spirits by labeling them demonic; and if we choose to label the souls of disembodied humans as demons, then we will have no choice but to believe we are encountering demons. The human experience has taught me that the mind makes real what it chooses to fearfully believe.

Another investigation in Canton, Ohio further confirmed my suspicions regarding demons and ghosts. Kate and Rob had purchased their ranch home in 2005. They noticed after moving into the house that each doorway had a black cross painted above it under the outside eaves. From the beginning, they sensed something might be eerily wrong within their newly acquired home. Kate and Rob chose to ignore their feelings about the house, thinking they were acting a bit paranoid. That approach didn't last long, because odd things began to happen to them that caused concern.

Some of the ghastly activity they experienced was disturbing. The haunting initially began with a back door uncharacteristically slamming shut on its own. Supernatural disturbances then manifested as a persistent knocking heard within the walls, a clicking sound continually emanating from within the home, Kate's jewelry rattling, coughing sounds coming from the hallway, and disembodied voices calling Rob's name. They noticed that the strange noises and unexplainable occurrences happened more in the evening when it was dark. Both Kate and Rob had been awakened at night by having their faces scratched: It made them quite certain that their residence was infested by demons. What didn't make sense to them was that Rob claimed he had witnessed the shadows of an older woman and a young girl walking around in the home.

"Could demons be masquerading as human spirits?" Rob asked us.

"I don't think so," I replied.

Kate and Rob continued to share their story with us. After

becoming very frightened by the horrible experiences, the couple had moved out of the home and put it up for sale. After a year on the market, the home had received no offers. This caused Kate and Rob to reluctantly move back in and see if the demonic activity had settled down. While laying in bed their first night back, they were abruptly interrupted with items from their dresser being knocked off, the feeling of someone touching them, and a pillow being held over Rob's face. An unseen entity did not want them there, and the couple was at their wit's end!

Being born-again Christians, Rob and Kate first attempted to request help from their church. After hearing the stories of what had taken place within the house, the church deemed the activity to be that of demons but refused to come out and help rid the home of its devils. To the church, ghosts were not even a consideration, because they do not believe in them. Remember that Christianity typically teaches that after a person's death, the soul is either whisked away to a blissful place called "Heaven" or cast into an eternal, fiery prison for torment known as "Hell." To the church leadership, the horrible activity experienced by Kate and Rob could only be the product of demons. Personally, I found it sad that the haunting frightened religious leaders who claim to possess truth about life and death. After the church's direct refusal to address the paranormal problem, *SIGHT* received a phone call asking if we would help. We, of course, welcomed such an opportunity.

Five or six of us arrived at night to listen to the stories about the haunting. We listened intently in the hope of determining what may have been occurring within the residence. Then, we split into two teams, deciding to investigate the upstairs and downstairs separately. While investigating, we paid attention to our intuition as well as our electronic instruments used for ghost detection. Not much of anything happened during our walk-through, which took an hour or so. Someone on the team did report hearing footsteps in the bathroom, but we couldn't be sure with so many people moving about the home.

I was of the mind that more movement in the home was actually better. I wanted to see if a group of people traipsing through the residence for hours would stir up any negative behavior. If the ghost was unhappy with Kate and Rob coming back to the house, I could only imagine how disturbing we must have been to the ghost as we investigated every room. Despite our best efforts, we struggled to capture anything by way of technical equipment or psychic intuition. I wondered if our ghost had decided to turn tail and run.

Being drawn to the master bedroom, I suggested we do a spirit circle there. Gathering around a candle in the darkness, we attempted to make contact by speaking to whoever might listen. When my turn came to speak, I followed my heart and attempted to say whatever came forth. I purposely directed my words toward the older lady whose shadow Rob had seen. His sighting of a ghostly woman offered us our best clue to solving the haunting, in my opinion.

After heading this direction for a while, Laura Lyn detected that an angry, older lady was there and trapping a young child with her for some unknown reason.

"Could this have been the young girl Rob had told us he saw?" I muttered under my breath.

Laura Lyn suspected that the girl wanted to cross over to the light and leave the home behind but was fearful of the older woman. The domineering matron was now angry with us. Her presence could be felt as heat on the back of my neck and chest, something I had encountered before with angry ghosts. Laura Lyn told us the ghost's name was "Mary." I elected to speak forcefully to Mary, demanding she leave the little girl alone so we could help her to the light. The young girl's fears then subsided, and she gently slipped into the light easily. A confirming presence of peace washed over some of us in the room.

Now, it was time to address Mary. Laura Lyn and another young psychic in the room were able to provide more details of what was bothering the earthbound spirit. It seems Mary was extremely upset about her husband who had died of cancer. After his passing, she found out he had been having an affair with another woman. Wanting revenge, she was bitter towards him and men in general.

Thinking I would be helpful, I called for Mary's husband as well as her mother. I thought that maybe the two of them might be able to help us reason with the angry ghost. With Laura Lyn acting as medium by allowing the ghost to speak through her, Mary shot back a disgusted retort to me.

"I don't want to see him!" This response made me chuckle and brought a lighthearted moment to the room.

"Will I be able to return and visit the home?"

"Yes, you will be freer than you are now...free to visit whomever you wish."

My answer to Mary shocked Kate and Rob who now wanted to insure things were set straight. They had mixed feelings about the spirit revisiting their home. We urged the couple to express to Mary how she had made them feel. I was eventually able to convince them to allow Mary to return from time to time, as the home meant so much to her.

"Please, do not make our lives a living hell any longer. You are welcome to visit from time to time as long as you honor our wishes by doing so without our knowing," Kate said.

Laura Lyn assured Kate and Rob that Mary understood their request and was grateful to them. Mary went into the light with her mother. She finally was at peace. The atmosphere in the small bedroom instantly transformed from negativity to a flow of love and joy. All of us felt the easing of tension, and we blessed the family before leaving at 2 AM. What a thrill to solve such a difficult haunting and one that had caused so much fear and torment.

When ghosts exhibit possessive behavior toward objects, places, or even people, they are often struggling with relinquishing a piece of their past. The ghost of Mary was just one example. I strain to make sense of the idea that ghosts are capable of literally "possessing" inanimate objects, as if they somehow inhabit them. Wouldn't it make more sense that a ghost might be emotionally attached to an item, occasionally becoming very protective of it? This I could see. Mementos from our past can be powerful stimulants in recalling our fondest of memories. Some ghosts might be unwilling to forget their past, determined to oversee personal objects, family members, or a former residence.

Like many communities, Chagrin Falls, Ohio has neighborhoods built on old farm pastures. The sprawling countryside now has become suburbs that are dotted with housing allotments. *SIGHT* was asked to investigate one of these houses. It was owned by a family haunted by an old man.

Besides hearing noises within the house, one of the children had witnessed balls of light hovering in his bedroom and in the basement. The young boy also had seen an older fellow dressed in overalls and sweeping the floor with a broom near the front door. He reminded him of his janitor at school.

Apparitions of people were not new to him, for the child had also seen his grandpa come visit him after he died while the family lived in their prior home. This time, the boy was frightened after hearing someone breathing close to his face while having his stuffed animal taken away from him. He no longer would sleep in his bedroom. I should mention he also saw the same old man floating in his parents' bedroom and heard a feminine-sounding voice calling his name. The boy's story reminded me of the movie *The Sixth Sense*.

The father of the family was not without his own strange experience. While working outside carrying a ladder, he noticed that one end suddenly became light as if he was being helped. When he asked whoever it was to stop lifting the end of the ladder, it immediately felt normal again. It was as if he had a caretaker with him.

The kitchen gained notoriety within the family for being the place to have items intentionally knocked from the grasp of people. In two separate incidences, a sugar bowl, and salt and pepper shakers were sent flying away from the hands that held them. Even a mother-in-law was witness to a tray having been pulled from somebody's grip and thrown to the counter. Needless to say, the family's lives were being disrupted and now their son was terrified. Something needed to change.

The accounts of the old man struck me as just an older gentleman who liked helping out. Perhaps, he was attending to things after his death and probably did not intend to be a bother. His interactions with the family did not appear to be malevolent but just misunderstood. I looked forward to meeting this spirit and seeing if we could help him.

As we walked upstairs, we were instantly captivated by a presence within the boy's bedroom. I was overcome almost instantly by a feeling of sadness as I entered the room. We immediately decided to make contact and help this gentleman head home. My compassion for him poured forth from my heart, and I knew he was there with me. He never meant harm to anyone but was simply watching over his former property.

Laura Lyn acted as a medium and channeled the male presence. His name was Charles, and his wife was with him, too. According to Laura Lyn, her name was Irene, and they had a story to tell. The housing developments had taken over his property, and he longed to clear it once again. Charles loved his land and didn't want to leave it behind, disliking the fact that it had been divided up for allotments. He longed to touch the soil as before, to work the fields that had been so much a part of his life.

Although it might have been difficult for him to hear, I needed to tell Charles that he was living in the past. Because he no longer had a body, he desired something in the physical world that he couldn't truly possess. With great patience, I reasoned with Charles about moving forward in his life-journey. I shared that he probably could own property once again and certainly would be reunited with family and friends who awaited him in the light. Even though I could tell this began to make sense to Charles, there was still reluctance on his part due to his wife. He didn't want to leave her behind.

Irene began to tell Laura Lyn that she had desired to be reunited with her daughter who was tragically taken from them while only three years old. She had been looking for her daughter and wondered why she could not find her in the same place they were at.

"Irene, she's in the light and calling for you," came bursting out of me. I knew I was speaking with authority. "You and Charles need to go into the light where she is at, take her hand, and head home together. Follow her voice and you will find her." Laura Lyn also affirmed this message to them.

Right away we could sense the family coming together and walking away in peace. The room was filled with a release of peace. Afterward, we shared our experience with the homeowners, making them aware that there was nothing more to fear. Two families found peace together in one evening.

My drive home was exhilarating as I thought about what a great work it is to rescue lost spirits. I thought to myself, "We need to make more people aware of how to do this and of its importance."

Chapter Six

We Are More Than Bodies

People are eternal energy. Although we may not realize it, we are much more than our visible persona. If our physical body were to expire today, who we are at heart would not change. Some call this invisible, human energy the "soul." The soul is an individual expression within a greater, all-encompassing energy of being that connects everyone and everything. This energy is often referred to by me as "spirit." We may view this greater energy of spirit to be our higher self, the enlightened source behind all matter.

I suspect that in order for people to have become conscious, unique individuals who materialized from within the greater energy, it first became necessary for each of us to see a reflection of our true, higher self.

"*...let us make mankind in our illusion, after our resemblance...*" - Genesis 1:26

The physical body is only a reflection of the real person. We know that the world around us acts as a mirror, allowing us to see and experience our individuality for a temporary period of time. I am proposing that this physical realm, which we have become very accustomed to, was necessary for our awakening to individuality. The material universe that appears to exist outside of us reveals what we need to see and experience in order to meet each individual's specific needs. There is little doubt that our time on earth allows us to learn important life-lessons; however, we also pay a price for such a valuable experience when we create a false persona due to our belief in the world reflected back to us. We might even think that titles and labels, as well as past successes and failures, can define our person. External experiences cause us to think the flesh body is all that we are, producing an egocentric illusion. This is how we might lose sense of our deeper being, the eternal connection to everyone and everything.

A time must come when the mirror that reflects the false is shattered, so we may see more clearly and return to the understanding of our eternal state. Death of the physical body is the shattering of the mirror, so to speak. Ultimately, we retain the things of value from this life and move beyond matters of little relevance. At least that's the way it should be for everyone. There are some who struggle with letting go of the past in order to move beyond the illusion. These people, if disembodied, walk among us as ghosts. All of us are individual expressions within the single, spirit energy. We are collectively having an earthly experience for a greater purpose that we often struggle to understand. A ghost simply continues to struggle with past experiences, even after the body's passing.

Having already touched on my own out-of-body experience, I think it is worthwhile to share more about the human soul's ability to temporarily disconnect from the physical form. An out-of-body experience, or OBE for short, typically occurs during sleep, meditation, or traumatic situations. The spirit energy of a person is somehow released from the body's hold on it, often floating up and away from the flesh. The separation of the soul from the body can happen in an instant and without warning. It is common for a person, who is experiencing an OBE to be able to look back and see their physical body lying still. Their faculties remain with them as they travel within the spirit energy. Although less common, it is also possible to have a spontaneous out-of-body experience (SOBE). An SOBE is when a person is active and unexpectedly steps out of their physical form for a moment, being aware of bilocation.

Sometimes during OBEs, people report hearing a buzzing sound in their ears, especially while leaving or returning to the body. Sight and sound remain active during the experience, but the ability to speak is, of course, hindered. There are no vocal chords to produce audible sound. The body lies dormant, often unable to move beyond a position of sleep.

The disembodied soul usually will return quickly to its physical shell as soon as the person thinks about their body. The process of regaining bodily control may actually take a few minutes. It is believed that the spirit animates the flesh and that somehow they remain connected during the out-of-body experience. This connection is sometimes referred to as the “silver cord,” a reference that goes back to an Old Testament Bible passage.

"Remember him–before the silver cord is severed, or the golden bowl is broken; before the pitcher is shattered at the spring, or the wheel broken at the well, and the dust returns to the ground it came from, and the spirit returns to God who gave it." - Ecclesiastes 12:6-7 (NIV)

I recall hearing the story of a young boy who experienced

being out-of-body. He had gone outside during recess at school to play with the other children. Being a snowy, winter day, the children were dressed warm and enjoyed chasing each other around the playground. While the young boy was running in the snow, he slipped on a hidden patch of ice. His feet left the ground and his small body slammed to the frozen earth with a loud "thud." Not long after, his playmates and an adult teacher made their way to the boy. They gathered around him as he lay on the ground unconscious. During this time, the boy's spirit floated above his friends and teacher. He silently observed their concerned faces and listened to their conversation about him. Then, he slipped back into his body and awakened to the crowd surrounding him. His out-of-body experience was something he would never forget. As an adult he would recount the story to me as if it were yesterday.

Accidental trips away from the body are one form of the phenomenon, but there are out-of-body experiences that are purposeful trips, too. These out-of-body experiences are welcomed and initiated through meditation. The practice is called "astral travel" or "astral projection." By relaxing the body until it is no longer recognized, it is possible for a person to mentally detach from their physical existence. With practice, the ability to allow one's soul to disconnect from the body becomes easier and easier. The awareness of the ethereal existence becomes heightened with each experience.

When a person is outside the body's limitations, they are able to travel wherever they desire. Some have told stories of traveling to loved ones, who live far away, to see them in spirit.

Others give account of visiting distant planets or even the higher and lower realms of human existence. It would seem there is no limit to where a person might choose to explore. Astral travelers have described encountering and speaking with enlightened spirits. Some spirit travelers, who have chosen to visit the lowest levels of human existence, have reported being terrorized by darker souls who seek others to intimidate. It would seem that the power of the mind to take a person wherever they desire is the key. The more debased the thoughts, the more depraved the destination. If the intentions of a soul are pure, then they will travel to higher states of ecstasy if desired.

Many years ago, an old friend of mine, Mike Cistone, shared his story of astral travel with me. Recently, I asked him to recount the story in his own words:

During a time when I was in the hospital for nearly one week, I began to have a series of experiences I describe as out-of-body journeys. These experiences continued for a while, and at one point, I actually felt I could initiate the event.

When I reflect back, I try to connect the circumstances that might explain these happenings; I'll attempt to repeat them here for you.

I have to start with a near death experience about six months earlier which may or may not have contributed to the beginning of these out-of-body episodes but remains as the first time I felt what I describe as my spirit leaving my body and returning. It was also the last time I would subject myself to the dangerous combination of drugs and alcohol that had rendered me nearly dead and which ultimately compromised my health to the point of requiring medical attention.

While in the hospital, it was common for the nurses to come into my room at very frequent intervals to draw blood for testing. This would continue, especially throughout the night, and it became difficult to sleep for many consecutive hours. It seemed like I was always awakened just as I entered deep sleep. I felt like I was suspended in a dreamlike time zone night after night.

The first time it happened, I naturally assumed that I was dreaming. I could see my room, my bed tray and all items in it, my sink and toilet included; but now my point of reference was not from my bed but from the ceiling. I saw these items as if I were floating on the ceiling like a helium balloon. After a brief time, I saw my own figure in bed, and it came zooming toward me. Actually, a better description is that I was falling toward myself; and the sensation of falling was very strong like the feeling you get in your stomach after the roller coaster you're riding peeks on the first giant hill and you plummet downward.

I can't recall how many times that week it happened, but it was several. I would wander against the ceiling, looking down, gradually expanding my journey to adjoining rooms and hallways. I was always strangely aware of the tops of doorways. These became small hurdles I learned to navigate with some effort by allowing myself to lower, cross over the top of the door jamb, and rise back up to ceiling level.

After I left the hospital, I continued to have these experiences from time to time but not as frequently as when I was a patient. I assume this was because I gradually was able to sleep continually without interruption. When I did have the experiences, they almost always came just before waking, and I was typically up at dawn or just before.

I experimented with consciously realizing this moment between waking and deep sleep in an effort to purposely take more of these flights which for me had become quite enjoyable and mystifying. I believed I could really fly, and occasionally I could capture this moment and float around. Then when I returned, it was always with the same stomach of butterflies associated with falling. Only once or twice do I remember leaving the confines of my own home to find myself floating in someone else's house.

This jabber all leads me to the really wonderful part of my experience. I had always kept this business to myself until one evening before going to bed (with a partner). I warned her, that if I appeared to be doing anything unusual in my sleep, not to be afraid; I had been experimenting with projection. After all, I didn't really know how it affected my sleeping body. That was all I said, and we went to sleep. We were in a room separate and downstairs from my sister's, whose house we shared. She was already asleep.

That night, or early in the morning, I had caught the moment just before waking and was able to enjoy another tour of the house while floating near the ceiling. Again, the tour would always end with the falling sensation and, then, waking.

That morning as we sat around the breakfast table, my sister began telling of her weird 'dream' from the previous evening. She claimed that she awoke, sat up in bed, and looked around the dark room where she saw me, legs crossed and arms folded across my knees, sitting near her dresser, smiling back at her. I just looked at my partner and watched her stunned expression as she remembered what I had told her the night before. I eventually explained to my sister what I was doing, and now she still wonders if she was dreaming or actually saw my wandering spirit.

Unfortunately, the out-of-body events gradually stopped. Perhaps I got lazy and decided I liked sleeping through the morning. Anyway, except for an occasional flying dream, I haven't had a so-called 'astral projection' in years. I was twenty-two at the time. I'm fifty-eight now, but I recall the feeling like it was yesterday.

Individual accounts of out-of-body experiences and astral travel further show that all of us exist together within an invisible energy. As a part of the whole of existence, we can never be disconnected from that energy, our source. This spirit of life is the core being of all that truly exists, the animating energy that lies at the heart of each soul. It is the essence of all. The truth is that everything is united by this invisible, all-knowing, all-encompassing, energy source. We simply need to become aware of it.

The idea that we could ever be separated from our source is simply a creation of our own misperception. Because we might not fully comprehend our complete nature, namely that we are much more than physical bodies of flesh and bone, mankind strives to find meaning from an external world that is passing away. Doesn't it sound ridiculous to desperately search the fading cosmos in an attempt to find eternal answers? If we focus solely on what we see happening outside of ourselves, then our mind will produce a feeling of separation, and we will believe we are disconnected from everyone and everything. We are left believing we live and die with the body, something quite fearful. Our existence becomes fleeting, and we deny that we are imperishable.

When we choose to view life using only the five senses, we see nouns: people, places, and things. Our mind is quick to assign labels to all that we see to attempt to make sense and order of it. I noted previously that such a mode of thinking produces fear within the mind. We especially fear the unknown. We can feel alone and small. "There must be something bigger, a god somewhere," we surmise. The idea of "god" then becomes a distant figure, too often pictured in our minds as an angry, judging deity seated on a throne somewhere high above the skies.

Should we take a moment to quiet the mind, we'll notice the deeper connection within our being. That vitality inside of us is the energy of unity, love, and peace; never fear. Some may call this "God," but I prefer to use the word, "spirit."

"God is Spirit..." - John 4:24

"Do you not know...the Spirit of God dwells in you?"

- I Corinthians 3:16

The spirit that gives all of us life is eternal, though we may remain unaware. This energy is who we are. If we listen to our heart, it is possible to know that we are not separate, nor are we lacking. Our connection with all of creation is as sure as our own perceived consciousness; therefore, death cannot separate us from this life-energy. In reality, there is no "other side of the grave." From this viewpoint, all of humanity can be perceived as being "one."

What is within us is also outside of us. Our frame of mind dictates what we believe. If our mind chooses to be enslaved to the idea of separation, then the world around us will appear divided. Death will then become something that separates us from our loved ones and something whose arrival we dread.

Truly, we experience what we create within our mind.

We read in the Bible that Jesus rejected belief in death, perhaps because he knew we are eternal spirits.

"'*Why all this commotion and crying? The child is not dead but sleeping.' But they laughed at him...*" - Mark 5:38-40

"*...let the dead bury the dead.*" - Matthew 8:22

We can learn to free ourselves from believing that we will become victims of death. No longer should we view a dying body as being greater than the eternal life that lies within the person. We needn't fall victim to our illusions about death and dying that we allow to be projected in our heads. We need to learn to see life and living.

It is the divine life source residing within us that works to free the mind of its false beliefs. I have heard that time heals all wounds. Wouldn't it be better, though, for times of suffering to be shortened whenever possible? The path inward is the way. If we choose to listen to what resides within, then the mind will come to eventually follow the elevated voice of reason. I have referred to this voice as our higher consciousness.

Even though we are living what may seem to be an individual human experience, we would do good to remember that we are not disconnected in any way. Allow me to convey this idea further. In *Kabbalah*, a mystical form of Judaism, there is a teaching that God chose to shatter like glass for a season. Each of us are individual shards of this sacred energy. Each piece of God is just as important as the next. It is taught that the fragments will eventually reassemble together as one and with new awareness. We are individual expressions of our eternal source, gradually uniting through an awakening to the truth: We are immortal spirit. Each soul, it would seem, is an essential part of the entire state of being. We can say there is an awakening of all humanity to harmony, and no one can be excluded. This is a party where everyone is invited and expected to arrive in their respective time.

It is fitting to consider the physical world as a place for the individualization of souls, a temporary playground to experience the lessons we need in order to come to the knowledge of truth. When we know our very existence can never be threatened, then fear subsides within us. The truth of the matter is that we are love, and we are loved.

Even though our lack of knowledge can produce suffering, I should mention that I feel it is our belief in good versus evil that is false. We think everything has to have an opposite. Namely, if there's a good, there must be a bad. I have found that belief in duality produces fear that causes suffering in me. Dualistic thinking is a symptom of mental separation, created through a lack of deeper awareness. In this world, we cannot help but feel a part of the chaos. This is natural. Still, we can also find the time to reconnect with the calming voice inside of us. This is healing. Have you ever considered, perhaps, that there may be only good? If everything is at work to collectively bring us to a greater consciousness, then how can any of it be bad, especially in light of eternity? If we consider that all of humanity is coming to an awareness of truth and knowledge regarding our oneness, then all paths, no matter how painful, can only be temporary and ultimately turning toward good. From an elevated vantage point, all must be good.

These ideas I share of oneness and goodness are important to understand so we do not succumb to fear. This brings me back to death of the body. Our physical existence, though it serves a purpose, has caused us to believe we've had a beginning; therefore, we might think we must have an end. Nothing could be further from the truth. While interacting in the midst of this world, it can be difficult to gain a much broader perspective on life. We may find that we have allowed death to cast a shadow of fear across our lives. This fear disconnects us from our higher knowledge of our incorruptibility.

Even when the body perishes, the real person lives on and is eternal. Our idea of death must be incorrect. If we continue living after our physical likeness has failed, then death cannot be real.

"O *death, where is your sting?* O *grave, where is your triumph?*" - I Corinthians 15:55

So what really is death? At the risk of sounding repetitive, death, to me, is when we are dead for a time to our true person, unaware of our incorruptible spirit. The true, whole person is a wellspring of peace and joy. Love already resides within us. Do we know this? Have we found the fount of joy and peace that bubbles forth inside? If we mentally disconnect ourselves from this eternal power, we consequently walk the earth like zombies fumbling around in darkness. Love, joy and peace may then seem fleeting.

When we do not know the power within us, our eternal

nature, then it is possible to be lost for a time. The mind creates illusions based upon interpreting the disconnected world it perceives it exists within and consequently reacts to anything it chooses to fear. I have expounded on disconnection and false perception in people who have bodies, because this mindset is no different for ghosts who do not have bodies. Like many of us, lost spirits are trapped in misbelief. They suffer for the same reasons we suffer. They are human.

Ghosts, to the fearing mind, are something to be left alone and not recognized as a part of who we are. Disembodied spirits are no different at heart than you or me. They are hurting people who have unfortunately fallen captive to the illusion of separateness, not yet aware of the depth of their eternal nature. Ghosts are enamored by the physical realm, frequently identifying strongly with their body that no longer exists. Their world appears separate, interpreted by the ghost as something to fear. It is fear ruling the ghost's mind like a cruel prison guard.

If you want to be a paranormal investigator, it is important to never fear ghosts. If fear holds us captive, how can we expect to free the minds of those who are also held captive by fear? Maybe you desire to be able to help earthbound spirits. Then it is best that you first help yourself. Do you know the truth of your deepest parts? Are you aware that you *are* eternal spirit energy, having nothing to fear? This is not my plea for people to become religious but a call to look deeper within your being until you know you are more than a body.

"*...the Kingdom of God is within you.*" - Luke 17:21

As you may have gathered by now from what you have read, there is depth to the human soul. Within us is the guiding compass of life. Becoming aware and guided by our inner voice of higher consciousness brings peace to us personally (keeping us from fear) and is our source of wisdom, love, and compassion that will touch the lives of others. We need to be in touch with our deepest source in order to access the tools necessary to be effective with helping ghosts.

Most of us are willing to help someone when they have a physical need, but it seems unconscionable that some ghost investigators will not consider helping those whom we do not see. We must come to recognize that unity, our oneness with everyone, must include those whom we do not see but, nevertheless, are with us. Where are the imaginary walls that separate ghosts and spirits from our existence? I tell you the walls only exist between our ears. Our definition of humanity must include benevolent, enlightened spirits as well as earthbound spirits, those whom we refer to as ghosts.

Most people are quite comfortable in believing that enlightened spirits, such as angels or spirit guides, coexist with mankind in order to bring comfort, timely messages, or even rescue during times of great need. Many want to believe that their deceased loved ones are far away in a peaceful land. That may be so for many of them, but are we to believe that there are no spirits that are in discomfort? What have we done with those who are with us who are suffering in the invisible? Do we even know they exist, or have we made them to be dead to us? Have we regarded lost spirits as being damned, undeserving of reconciliation?

My studies and experiences have caused me to ask myself many questions about what I had not really considered. Could it be possible, whether we like it or not, that ghosts are just as much a part of us as those who are enlightened? Have we included the unseen hurting and lost as a part of our personal definition of everyone? Have we constructed fictitious walls within our minds that have shut traumatized spirits out? Are we unknowingly picturing the dead as being somewhere far away from us? If our beliefs about the dead have been wrong, then what are we going to do about it?

Sharing the same eternal energy, all of us should want to help others overcome their fears. We are not alone in this ideal. By working together with others in spirit who share the same desire to help all of humanity, we can reach those who are temporarily stuck in transition. Ghosts are people, like you and me, who are on a journey toward understanding truth. They have simply become trapped in the illusion and need help moving beyond their beliefs. Let's bring them truth.

Chapter Seven

The Ghost Mind

The human mind is powerful. It possesses the ability to make things appear real even when they are not. Like a scene from a movie, illusions created by the mind can cast a person deep into a false setting with seemingly no way out.

Our dreams are obvious examples of just how powerful the mind can be. All of us have had dreams that remained in our memory for a time after waking, due to how real the images and events appeared to be. We rationalize and try to understand our most powerful dreams, captivated by how an illusion could be so deceiving.

"How can you prove whether at this moment we are sleeping, and all our thoughts are a dream; or whether we are awake, and talking to one another in the waking state?" - Plato

Great philosophers such as Aristotle and Plato studied the dream phenomenon and the power of the human mind. It was Plato who drew the conclusion that the human mind sometimes behaves like an out-of-control beast on the prowl during times of sleep. Aristotle thought there might be a similarity found among mental illness, fantasies, illusions, and dreams. He observed that animals, like human beings, dream. Similar to the journey we experience while on earth, dreams appear to be temporary illusions that serve some sort of purpose.

Interestingly, *The Tibetan Book of the Dead* describes death as being similar to the dreamlike state. According to the texts, the death experience may be pleasant or fearful depending on our beliefs. Death is viewed as a process that reveals the nature of what we are thinking, beliefs being something we need liberated from. Feelings of hatred, anger, pride, greed, concern, overachievement, paranoia, and self-seeking are just some of the mind's snares that we need to eventually overcome. The journey toward recognizing and dispelling false beliefs might be described as entering into insanity in order to grasp hold of enlightenment.

Beliefs can become powerful barriers within the mind. Through our interaction within the physical environment, we establish various opinions about ourselves, others, and the world in general. Beliefs are not the same as knowledge. We believe when we do not know, creating views based upon our experiences. When beliefs become established within the human mind, they can be very difficult to uproot, even when they are incorrect. We simply do not like to let go of things we thought we had figured out.

I recall a time when I believed in Santa Claus. My belief in the jolly, old elf was taught to me by my parents. Because I thought my parents always told me the truth, I had no reason whatsoever to doubt their word or the confirmation of countless others. The day eventually came when my mother had decided it was time to tell me that Santa Claus was a fictional character. At first I argued with her, choosing not to believe her. I simply could not wrap my brain around the idea that my mom had fooled me. When I was finally able to understand that I had been deceived, I became very angry. I remember telling my mom that she had made me look like a fool to others. I cried for quite some time, shocked and saddened that I had not been told the truth. As a little boy, I would rather have known the truth than believed a lie.

Ghosts are the product of not knowing truth. Many unenlightened spirits are unaware that they are eternal spirit energy, believing false things about themselves and others. The world the ghost operates within is a place of good and bad, separation, lack, and sometimes punishment.

In my opinion, ghosts are people in hell. Hell is often taught to be a place of punishment, and, in a sense, it is a place. The mind has created a place of torment for the ghost, something that is false. At any given time it is possible for them to step out of the illusion. Ghosts remain unaware that their condition is caused by a correctable state of mind that has become self-induced suffering. As if they were within a carnival's house of mirrors, ghosts wander about, struggling to find the way out.

What a person experiences is primarily the result of their thinking. We often do not understand this, because we live our lives in fear, believing that we are either the victims or the benefactors from everything that takes place outside of ourselves. Our years spent on earth have taught us to trust what our five senses deliver to the brain as validation of what is real. We must rely upon things that we seem to have no control over.

I mentioned several times that focusing our lives only on

external images produces fear we must eventually overcome. We might not want to recognize what lies beneath the surface. Our inner fears can remain hidden until they decide to manifest to torture the mind. We must choose to come out of our self-created dungeon. The depth of the cellar we create is equal to the depth of the illusion. What we bury within us will be revealed on the other side of the grave when this world is pulled out from under our feet. A soul can become unable to move forward in life, remaining trapped in the past and tormented in the present by the mind. This emotional turmoil, rooted in fearful beliefs, is hellish.

"...there is nothing covered that shall not be revealed, and hid that shall not be known."

– Matthew 10:26

A person who dies while in a good state of mind will find their way to the light and transition forward to continue their unique life-journey quite easily. They gladly accept the greeting by loved ones while basking in the cleansing light and embracing a deep peace which is now theirs. A life-review quickly ensues. The past is settled and the entire universe is made right in the mind, once again. I think the cleansing process of the mind is much like a computer having its hard drive cleaned up. It corrects errors in the reasoning process. This is the path we should all choose to embrace.

Ghosts have, for various reasons, rejected the light and beckoning of loved ones. Perhaps, they were unable to see the illuminated path forward or maybe they feared what might lie ahead. Others might have been focused on people or places in their past and were not ready to leave it all behind. No matter the reason, their choice has caused them to become a shadow of the complete person for a time.

Some ghosts do not know they are dead. They feel very much alive and do not recall having a death experience. The world does seem different to them, but their mind is not initially able to come to terms with what has happened. This is typically the case with ghosts whose bodies expired suddenly and before their time on earth was deemed complete. Trauma produced from untimely deaths, such as murder, sickness, physical abuse, drug overdose, and so on, can leave a soul lost in transition. Some ghosts may subconsciously choose not to remember painful events and emotionally shut down. Ghosts who have experienced a sudden death often wander their former haunts looking for answers. They find no one to hear their pleas for help. Eventually, they will make progress toward understanding their condition.

I shared that not every ghost wants our help. Many are somewhat aware of their current state and quite content to remain that way for awhile. Still, all ghosts certainly deserve our help navigating through the quagmires they have unwittingly created through the power of their own mind. Although help might not be requested by ghosts, and sometimes it is refused, the ghost mentality is still one of needless suffering. This is why I am making a plea for those who do not have a voice or may not know any better. If they could see that what lies ahead of them is much grander than their current circumstance, I am convinced most all would choose to move on unto better pastures.

Many ghosts do want our assistance. Certainly, we can agree to at least help those who welcome our direction. Some will even beg for it. Ghosts frequently remain desperate for any bit of communication offered by people whom they are attempting to reach. Their endeavors may go undetected. As the years roll by, ghosts seem to lose a sense of time, and their unending attempts to be noticed often result in frustration. A haunting generally goes unperceived until a discouraged ghost's efforts to make contact with fellow humans becomes something that even a skeptic would recognize as unordinary. Strange behavior is why ghostly visitation is often misinterpreted as something frightening or devilish.

Imagine, if you will, that your mouth suddenly disappeared. In fact, let's say that your entire body just vanished. Yet, you are still in a familiar setting and very much alive. You begin to wonder if you have died. You know you are alive, because you are consciously aware that something has happened to you. You are now afraid and feel you must find someone to help you. How will you communicate with people when you find them? How will you get their attention? You don't know, but you reason that you'll figure it out when the time comes. Your mind begins to think of things that you have left unfinished. You wish you could have said goodbye to family and friends. Panic sets in at this point, so you try to not think about what you might have missed out on. It is then that you realize you have been floating helplessly about the room. Struggling, you make an attempt to direct your movements with the power of your mind. There is no muscle to propel you. Feeling yourself slowly move about the room, sooner or later you make your way to a place where there are people.

As a ghost, you might try to pass through the first person you see, but your attempt is only thought to be a draft in the house. As numerous tries to communicate through touching and speaking go unnoticed, you become frustrated, even angry. You repeatedly try to speak with family for what may seem like days. Actually, months have passed, and you have lost all sense of time. You wonder if you are trapped within a bad dream, something you hope to awaken from. You've now had a long time for reflection, and you decide to think outside the box about how you might reach loved ones, or anyone for that matter, who might recognize your plight. You attempt different things, what some may deem as "crazy." You know you are still alive, but now what? Where do you go? What do you do? What lies ahead of you? Do you even have a future?

Given more time, you begin to figure out how to use the power of your mind even though you still believe lacking flesh is a disadvantage. Similar to when you were once an infant, you familiarize yourself with a new world and relearn how to function without physical form. There's no point in attempting to operate like you did when you had a body. That way of thinking will not work for you any longer. Although you had ideas of how to make contact with people, now you have become more capable of doing so.

Perhaps, appearing to people in dreams, yelling in someone's ear, or moving personal possessions are now options to gain someone's attention as you become more adept with your abilities. The stronger your intentions become, the more you are able to do. It is possible to reach through the veil from one realm to the next. Maybe, you can even share your thoughts with another in the same room or attempt to become connected with a person's body if given the right scenario. If you could move their mouth and speak through them, others could hear you. At this point, you are determined to stop at nothing until your dilemma ends. Eventually, you know you'll find answers that bring peace. This is your resolve.

I have become convinced that ghosts are simply misconstrued. How could we ever fully comprehend their peculiar position? We should conclude, then, that ghosts are largely misunderstood, occasionally frustrated, lost spirits of people.

Our ideas concerning ghosts might have become distorted. Allow me to give you an example. Take a moment and examine the illustration on the front cover of this book. How do you perceive the image? Is this a picture of a scary ghost reaching out to grab you, or is the hand desperately grasping for help, searching for any lifeline? How you choose to view this illustration might indicate what you have chosen to believe about disembodied spirits of fellow human beings.

Now, perhaps, you know why I become frustrated with television programs that show ghost hunters capturing ghost evidence, even cries for help, then abandoning the lost spirits after attempting to communicate with them. Some investigators even hurl insults to provoke earthbound spirits, looking for a reaction that proves their existence. Those of us who embark upon paranormal investigation have got to become more understanding of the ghost condition, allowing compassion to become the motivator behind our actions.

Sometimes being a good listener is all that is required to ease the mind of a human spirit. Plenty of ghosts do wish to communicate or relay messages to loved ones, being very willing to resolve past issues. We can help them. The more I work to understand the behavior of ghosts, the more I come to realize that we must remain open to every possible reason the spirit of a person may remain behind. The key to worthy ghost investigation, then, is to become a compassionate listener.

A good number of ghosts are too afraid to move beyond the only world they have known. Interacting with the earth's inhabitants provides a level of comfort for them. The more time they can spend with people they have bonds with, the better they feel and remain at ease. Some ghosts actually feel part of a family. It is certainly nice to hear of people who appreciate and welcome the souls of relatives or friends into their homes. Such an expression of love does help to abate the ghost's fears for a time; however, eventually the ghost needs to move onward to experience true healing. There is no hiding from fear. All fears we elect to keep will, in time, be exposed.

The intensity of the fear the disembodied spirit suffers can vary depending on the beliefs they learned while in-body. What could a ghost possibly believe awaits them that could be so terrifying? It's something anyone might feel from time to time, a form of fear known as guilt. Whether we realize it or not, we may feel guilty for things we have done in the past. After the body expires, guilt and fear will eventually surface and should be dealt with; otherwise, the mind will believe in a foreboding future. I have already mentioned that ghosts sometimes fear judgment for past mistakes. Imagine reuniting with someone you have disappointed such as a parent who died before you? You might wonder if they forgive you. Upon meeting them again, would you look forward to possibly facing embarrassment, scolding, or even worse, rejection? Think about the spirits of people who have purposely or inadvertently taken human lives. Would they welcome the opportunity to face their victims? In most cases, I would think not. Naturally, they would want to postpone such traumatic reunions, hoping they might still find forgiveness.

Having already shared some of my thoughts about Western religion and its teaching, I wish to further expound upon the idea of Hell and judgment. You now know that the light itself can be perceived by ghosts as the place where they will meet their final judgment from an angry god. The ghost might even equate the light with being the flames of a harrowing Hell, a place where one must pay the price for all prior misdeeds. For these reasons, the light of healing becomes something that must be rejected and hidden from due to feelings of unworthiness and condemnation. If people who believe in Hell die in their guilt, then every mistake they have made in life could be misinterpreted as sins that demand settlement with a condemning god who demands appeasement. These thoughts operating in the mind of the self-condemned become the demons that pursue them in the darkness while they hide in shame. The misrepresentation of God by religion has created more lost souls than can be imagined, saving very few in the process.

"Woe to you religious leaders...for you walk around land and sea to gain one convert, and when he is gained, you turn that convert into double the child of hell as yourselves!" - Matthew 23:15

From what I have been able to deduce, judgment is something that we bring upon ourselves. No one is better at laying condemnation upon me than me. I have noticed that condemnation only exists in the past and not in the present day. If we are feeling condemned and judged, it is because our mind is being held captive to the past and not living in this very moment.

The condemnation that ghosts feel is self-created and perpetuated through their own mind, too. They are still living in a time that has passed. Wayward spirits are often unable to understand that they are the only ones carrying their past mistakes with them into the present. This causes ghosts to fear their future. Forgiveness is letting go of the past. Forgiving one's self is paramount, as true forgiveness allows us to forget our errors and move beyond them.

I often share with people the parable about forgiveness found within the Bible. It is typically used to teach about forgiveness of others. Although it is certainly healing to forgive other people, to me, the passage reveals that forgiving ourselves is the key to our personal freedom.

"Settle matters quickly with your adversary who is taking you to

court. Do it while you are still with him on the way, or he may hand you over to the judge, and the judge may hand you over to the officer, and you may be thrown into prison. I tell you the truth; you will not get out until you have paid the last penny." - Matthew 5:26

The judgment takes place within each individual. We are the judge who is capable of sentencing and imprisoning ourselves. Prisoners in this jail will remain condemned until they feel they have paid whatever debt necessary to relinquish their guilt. Those who remain under self-condemnation are unaware that every soul possesses the key to being released. We can leave our self-imposed penitentiary at any moment. We only need to forgive ourselves to end our suffering.

"Therefore whatsoever you have spoken in darkness shall be heard in the light...be not afraid of them that kill the body and after that have no more they can do. I shall forewarn you whom you shall fear. Fear him, which after he hath killed, has the power to cast you into suffering..." - Luke 12:3-5

Some ghosts believe the condemnation they suffer is from God. They await and hope for forgiveness to come from a higher power outside of them; then, their healing does not arrive. Forgiveness can only come from within by forgiving others as well as ourselves. Ghosts must learn to forget past mistakes and move beyond them. Otherwise, they will remain seeing themselves separate, lacking, and deserving of punishment.

Because of their fears, ghosts tend to hide under the cover of evening. They may fear being punished or fear being seen by other people. Ill-intentioned ghosts will also prefer to hide within darkness; if a ghost wants to invoke fear, then darkness is a benefit. Occasionally, paranormal investigators will say it's foolish to believe tales of ghosts coming out at night. I agree with them to a point. From different accounts of ghost activity, we know that spirits may choose to interact with people whatever time they like. Still, there always seems to be bits of knowledge hidden within superstitions. Darkness does offer benefits for a ghost who does not wish to be detected; it provides the perfect cover to mask their presence.

I have shared that darkness is a symptom of condition and not an indicator of evil. It has also been my contention that light may be described as truth, something that can be tangibly felt as a great love, peace, and joy within us. I must reiterate that darkness, on the other hand, represents a temporary inability to comprehend the light of truth; it is a manifestation of fear, no matter the form. Fear, such as guilt, doubt, worry, condemnation, anger, attack, and the like, is the common theme found present within every ghost mind. Even remaining unaware and feeling lost is a form of fear that may manifest visibly as darkness. In short, we are beings of love. Anything that we believe contrary to our true nature is caused by fear darkening our ability to understand. Fear is the result of not understanding there is nothing to fear.

"And the light shines in darkness and the darkness did not comprehend it." - John 1:5

"If your vision is impaired, then your whole body shall be full of darkness. If therefore the light within you is darkened, how great is that

darkness!" - Matthew 6:23

"Take heed, therefore that the light which is in you is not darkness. If therefore your whole body is full of light, having no part of the dark, the whole shall be full of light..." - Luke 11:35-36

"Walk while you have the light, lest darkness come upon you. For he that walks in darkness does not know where he is going." - John 12:35

Hell is darkness, the fearing mind of a person independent of their location, whether in-body or not. The condition of our mind, while on earth, will be the condition of our soul when we leave the body behind. What have you already chosen to believe about yourself? We are what we believe until we choose to let go of the ideas we possess that are false.

As you have learned through reading some of my ghost investigation stories, sometimes ghosts do exhibit negative behavior but so do most people. To me, human behavior is quite similar to ghost behavior. The only difference between the two is how we choose to interpret the actions. When two different worlds come in contact with one another, we must keep in mind that the thought behind the action might be the same; however, the action may need to be interpreted differently.

We can imagine that if there are Type A personalities of people in this world, then there are certainly ghosts that also exhibit Type A tendencies. What do I mean by "Type A"? Type A and B personalities are from a theory that describes human behavior. Type A people are believed to be more dominant, time-oriented, stressed, and typically aggressive, perhaps due to low self-esteem. Type B personalities are more easygoing and relaxed, choosing to plod through life as it comes. In theory, other personalities can then be grouped as a mixture between A and B.

Ghosts seem to also exhibit these same personality traits. Type A personality describes ghosts that are controlling of others, aggressive, impatient, and angry. If someone is truly terrorized in their own home by a ghost, it is usually by a very controlling, mean-spirited person who seeks to dominate others around them. Most ghosts do not behave this badly, but some do.

The need for control is an interesting behavior found within the animal and human psyche. When an animal, such as dog, is placed within a group of other animals, it will look to determine who is in charge of the pack. If no one is clearly identified as the leader, then typically that animal will assume the leadership role in order to bring some sort of control and order to the situation.

Human beings are no different. When we gather with other people, we subconsciously attempt to determine who is leading the group. We search for order. In the workplace environment, things get done; because we rely upon leaders to direct the business. School systems have teachers who instruct students and maintain order within classrooms. So, it should not be shocking to learn that ghosts also look for order. Sometimes, they submit to the authority with them in their setting. This could be a person they respect, such as a homeowner, or another ghost whom they might even fear. It also means it is possible for ghosts to sometimes work to control an environment, a household, a person in-body, or even other ghosts. When working with lost spirits, I have experienced multiple ghosts cross over to the light at the same time. This was especially true after a controlling ghost, who tormented others through fear, decided it was time to leave first.

Interestingly enough, Dr. Edith Fiore shared in her book, *The Unquiet Dead*, that she also discovered this phenomenon while doing past life regression through hypnosis with her patients. What she first thought were memories of previous experiences left over from other lifetimes, ended up being intelligent, disembodied, human spirits somehow attached to her patients. The personalities, fears and demeanor of the ghosts were affecting their hosts negatively. Dr. Fiore, at times, would find only one ghost linked to the patient. Yet, she soon found it common for several ghosts to have become attached and living with the suffering person. This was especially true in the more severe cases. When Dr. Fiore was able to identify the most dominant ghost who controlled the others, she would work to convince him or her that it was time to move to the light and be with loved ones. The other ghosts often would then feel relieved and soon follow suit. They did not wish to remain behind but had become trapped with the host and afraid of the domineering spirit.

Through various ghost investigation cases I have been a part of, I have learned that, sometimes, negative ghosts are unintentionally invited to visit the unsuspecting during attempts at communication with the dead. Occasionally, a domineering ghost may find someone to haunt who has decided to use an *Ouija Board* or attempted to communicate with ghosts through other methods such as recording EVP. It's not that communicating with ghosts and spirits is wrong. It's just not something you should attempt to do if you are vulnerable to fear.

I can think of two different cases of negative ghosts ruling people and households, and both of them began to occur while the victims were grieving and trying to communicate with their recently departed loved ones. The state of mind of the grieving is weakened, apparently making them more vulnerable to negative ghost attacks. The perfect target for a scheming ghost, people suffering grief can be more open to believing any form of communication might be a sign from their deceased loved one.

Not only grief, but illness, can also allow a person to become open to ghost attacks by a degenerate entity. Take note that whatever debilitates the mental state, such as excessive use of drugs or alcohol, can also diminish a person's resistance to an attack. A ghost with ill intentions will attempt to invoke fear in those who are weakened mentally, physically, and willing to believe them. It is not uncommon for negative ghosts to manifest as frightening forms in order make them appear more menacing. If they can frighten a person, then this allows the ghost to assume control and dominate the weaker mind, either through torment or even attachment.

I do not wish to frighten anyone, but I think it is best to be aware of worst-case scenarios. Ghosts can become focused upon a person's life and become attached. Ghost attachment is also known as "possession" and is often mistaken for demon possession. As I have alluded to prior, there are no demons other than the negative thoughts our minds sometimes create and believe to be real. Ghost attachment, on the other hand, is real, even though many seem unaware of it. The degree of attachment and control a negative ghost has over another is directly related to the amount of fear suffered by the victim. A mind full of fear can allow a ghost to almost completely dominate the person's life to the point of altering their behavior.

Recently, I tuned into a popular ghost investigation television show that featured exorcism. The spirit was wreaking havoc upon a family. It seemed that because the entity was extremely mean-spirited, the investigators and team "demonologist" immediately labeled the behavior as demonic activity. Eventually, they performed an exorcism on the husband in an attempt to rid him of his demon.

The last decade has seen a tremendous interest in the paranormal, spawning the creation of many so-called "demonologists." Of course, I do not share these beliefs and think the emergence of the demonologist has evolved out of fears created by religion. If a person is bothered by a villainous ghost, it is better to lessen the fear, not intensify it. Fear is the ghost's weapon to gain control. To call a ghost a "demon," especially while trying to perform an exorcism, will oftentimes only make matters worse. An exorcism may cause the ghost to leave but likely only from tiring of the fight. It is possible to make an ill-mannered ghost feel even mightier by labeling the specter a demon! The ghost will know that pretending to be a demon is more frightening to people than simply being a human spirit with bad behavior.

Ghosts who wish to enact revenge upon another, or even whole families, are very common in some cultures. It is as if the invisible attacker and the victims believe it to be warranted due to superstitious beliefs and past sins of the family. I recall a very nice Hindu lady from overseas, who wrote me, asking for help. She explained in her e-mail letter that her family was suffering from what she called "serious ghost issues." Claiming that her entire family had been cursed by an angry man who had died decades earlier, she explained that his revenge was justified; because the man's suffering was caused by one of her family members. Her letter further described how even the family's innocent children were now bearing the wrath of several ghosts, possibly disembodied relatives of the angry man. She related to me how some of them even suffered from what she called "ghost possession." The battle with these ghosts had left them tired, very depressed, and desperate for my advice.

I wrote her back and suggested she approach the situation with compassion by first apologizing for her relative's past mistake and asking for the ghosts' forgiveness. I also encouraged her to tell the ghosts that she wanted them to have peace in their own lives by being reunited with their loved ones who awaited them in spirit. She wrote me later to inform me that my response had helped her change her mind "from anger to understanding and, hopefully, to love." Challenging ghost problems are easier to resolve when we choose to respond with actions based out of love and not reactions caused by fear.

Negative ghosts can also become attracted to people with similar passions or habits. Some earthbound entities pursue unsuspecting people in an attempt to become attached, hoping to once again experience a shared addiction such as sex, alcohol, or drugs. The high that the host feels may also be felt by the hidden, parasitic ghost. Sometimes, the ghost attachment can become very strong and even dominate the addict's personality. This type of negative behavior can be devastating and make the situation seem hopeless for the victim. If unable to find a human host to manipulate like a puppet, a ghost with a tyrannical demeanor will still harass people. If sexually perverted, the ghost may try and prey upon a target even without a body.

One unfortunate lady, who contacted me, described her invisible, sexual attacker as "a man who rode on her back." Nightly, the degenerate ghost would sexually assault her to the point she no longer found it possible to sleep. The poor woman was repeatedly told by the perverted ghost that he would never let her go. Being weakened and tired from the oppressive spirit, she believed him. Through fear, the ghost gained greater power and control over her. When she threatened to seek help, the possessive spirit offered to leave if she would help him attach to her friend. The woman denied the ghost's request, and the attacks continued. Last I heard, the exhausted lady opted to try professional counseling and medication in an attempt to suppress the ghost.

In *Kabbalah*, it is sometimes taught that ghosts can attach or "cling" to people. A *dybbuk*, Hebrew for "clinging spirit," is traditionally removed through talking with the wayward spirit, coupled with the ceremonial blowing of a ram's horn trumpet, called a *shofar*. Communication with the attached spirit is initiated in order to help the ghost resolve all unfinished, earthly business. Afterward, the ghost is willing to leave. It is believed that communicating not only helps to heal the soul of the clinging ghost but also frees the person who has suffered the spirit attachment.

An example of spirit attachment in the Hebrew Bible reveals that ghosts can affect the behavior of others. We read King Saul was vexed by a clinging, human spirit.

"...and the injurious spirit...came forcefully upon Saul. Saul had a spear in his hand and hurled it (at David)." - excerpted from I Samuel 18:10-11

I would contend that ghost attachment is often mistakenly thought to be demon possession. Being misinformed, some paranormal investigators of Western culture tend to believe they are dealing with a malevolent demon whenever a ghost with a mean disposition is encountered. Confronting such a situation can be frightening. Not sure what to do, the response may be to call for a Catholic exorcism performed by a priest. This type of exorcism may appear to be successful by temporarily driving a ghost away from a person, but more often than not, they provoke anger, making the spirit more determined to bring harm to the victim. It is not uncommon for ghosts that have been driven away to revisit the former host awhile later.

"When an unclean spirit has left a person...he seeks rest; and finding none, the spirit says unto himself, 'I will return to my dwelling where I left.'" - Luke 11:24

If a ghost is forced to leave through a Catholic exorcism, the suffering spirit is not healed and is likely to return or pursue another unsuspecting victim. The reason for this is because religious icons and ritualistic methods used for exorcism are effectually powerless. For these rites to hold any power at all, the ghost must fear godly retribution and thus feel compelled to obey the priest's commands in some fashion. Often to avoid further trouble, the ghost will simply pretend to have permanently left in order to quietly return later to its accustomed behavior. When negative ghosts appear to quiet down or leave, they often do so in order to stop the interruption of their normal activities. As a ghost investigator, if you choose to one day work with people who suffer from negative ghost activity, know that it may require repeated efforts to eventually resolve each particular situation.

Have you ever noticed the accounts in the Bible of Jesus talking with unclean spirits? If these spirits were of no value, why would he take the time to talk with them? You won't find him using holy water or crucifixes to drive out ghosts. We read that he spoke to them. This is important to understand, because communication is the path to healing. In one example, we read of Jesus speaking with lost, human spirits from the time of the Great Flood. It's important to note that the author of Genesis 6:5-7 calls the people who died by flood waters, "evil." If these evil, human spirits were condemned to an eternal hell, as some

Christian teachings would have us believe, then why would Jesus take the time to speak with them? The answer is to free them.

"...he also went and preached to the spirits in prison which were disobedient...in the days of Noah." - I Peter 3:19-20

Communicating with the unlovable is what frees the lost. Although negative entities can be controlling and mean, they deserve our help. The job may not be easy because of their personality and their ability to resist those who have their best interest at heart. Most negative ghosts are very adept at manipulating people and things. They may even partially understand their own ghastly condition, knowing they have chosen to become ghosts by hiding from the light. Some enjoy frightening others around them, whether it is other ghosts or people they are persecuting in their own homes. It is a mistake to allow mean-spirited people, including ghosts, to control us through fear. We have the ability to put our foot down and not be swayed by such attacks.

I had found myself wondering why a person in spirit might be mean to others. What do they get in return, except maybe the pleasure of being in control over another? The answer is that ill-mannered ghosts attack, because it makes them feel better about themselves. Truthfully, hurting people hurt others. If we lower someone in our mind by degrading them, we subconsciously believe we are elevating our self. We temporarily feel better. When we exhibit any type of self-destructive behavior, the truth is we enjoy the short-lived sense of joy it brings. We want to feel loved. Because this feeling is fleeting, we learn to repeat the negative behavior over again like a drug addict looking for the next high. The cycle will continue until we come to realize that the love and joy we think we lack has been with us the entire time. It's just been covered up within the depths of our soul. Disconnecting from it has caused us to feel less than whole and deprived. Finding that source deep down, and connecting to it, brings us back to wholeness.

I do not wish for you to become afraid of negative people in spirit. Be aware that negative ghosts do exist but are not the norm. When ghosts attack people, let's remember that it is because they are also hurting inside. It is possible to help ghosts overcome their issues. To do so, we should not combat mean spirits. Use of anger and vulgarity is not fruitful, either. Attacks may only aggravate and provoke some ghosts into retaliation. I already shared how people have reported being pushed, smothered, or even clawed by furious entities.

Every imaginable mental state we might encounter in a ghost is the result of their own choices that have caused them to suffer; therefore, peace evades them. Ghosts do not have a favorable impression of themselves, because they are not fully aware of the good that lies within them. We can deduce, then, that fear is the driving force behind a ghost's actions. Use of fear will not undo fear in another, nor will attacks of any kind help their situation. It is not possible to force a ghost's deranged mind to lessen its grasp on itself and be free. Helping ghosts really depends on understanding one main idea: Alleviate their fear, and you will free them. Only love, nothing else, can release a depraved soul from its own fearful grasp.

Chapter Eight

How Can We Help?

For some who may read this book, the thought of helping ghosts might seem foreign. I must admit that the idea is somewhat radical in itself and something I could not have fathomed had I not experienced the events that I have detailed within these pages. After sharing some of my experiences and findings, let's take a look at how we might put them into practice.

How can you determine if there is a ghost around you or your family who might be in need of your help? There is no simple litmus test you can perform. You must rely upon your own observations. First, consider if you have noticed anything out of the ordinary that has occurred within your environment. Has anything odd happened that you might have ignored? Have you felt cold spots in any of the rooms you frequent or goose bumps that come and go for no apparent reason? Has there been an electrical disturbance, such as appliances turning on or off by themselves, phone calls with no one on the other end of the line, or flickering lights? What about nonelectrical disturbances, such as toilets flushing, doors opening or closing on their own, or water fixtures turning on by themselves? Have any personal items recently disappeared or been moved, only to reappear back in a spot you've already searched? If you have experienced any of these examples, your house could be haunted.

What about phantom noises? Have you heard whispers, your name called, footsteps, knocking, unexplained music, or other odd sounds that you cannot explain? Did you notice any unusual odors, such as the fragrance of flowers or the aroma of cigars, that might be attributed to someone you know who is deceased? Do you have a dog or cat that is behaving strangely at times, such as barking at something you do not see? Have your eyes caught a glimpse of moving shadows, balls of light, or mists that were peculiar? Most importantly, do you know someone who recently passed around the time you first noticed the strange phenomena? Has this person appeared in any of your dreams?

The questions I pose are not all-inclusive but just some ideas of what to look for beyond the obvious. Some might think they have to see an apparition to know a ghost is present. This is not always the case. Active ghost haunting is sometimes overlooked even when it occurs right under one's nose. Be willing to accept the improbable. Consider if there is someone, anyone around you that could be trying to gain your attention. Have you been oblivious to it? If there has been any inexplicable activity within your home, could it be an attempt to startle someone who might listen? Should a ghost want to catch your attention, then the activity will likely be something out of the ordinary, maybe even frightening. This is why ghost behavior appears to be inordinate: it is meant to garner attention!

You have learned that paranormal phenomena can become repetitive. Examples of this might be repeatedly hearing the same mysterious sound or seeing the same see-through man walking down a flight of stairs, over and over again. If there is a repetitious, paranormal phenomenon that is not responsive to the living, it is possible that the environment has somehow kept record of a past event, making it visible or audible through a window in time. This type of ghost might not interact with people in this plane; but don't be too quick to think that an unresponsive haunting must be residual energy. It is also possible that the ghost is trapped in a severe state of mental trauma from the past and has tuned-out people, places, and things in the present. Such ghosts could be walking around in a stupor, interacting within a hallucination that only they can see. We might need to think out of the box with a ghost found in this condition. The goal would be to attempt to awaken the entity from its nightmare. If the ghost interacts with the present day at all, then the apparition is not the result of a residual haunting.

Disruptions in a home, including redecorating or remodeling of the house structure, can stir up the activity of ghosts and make them known. Spirits who are fond of a certain place seem very willing to express any resentment toward changes occurring within their environment. Think of it as a protest. Some ghosts believe that a residence is still their home and can become very protective of places, items, even people. It is not uncommon for ghosts to be attracted to strangers they share a common interest with or an inanimate object from their past life that still carries special significance. Any change within a ghost's favorite habitation could spark a disruption in their illusion, their day to day pattern of what they might find comforting.

When determining whether or not a person is experiencing an active haunting, we must remain aware that the human mind can become frenzied, creating situations that are very believable and seemingly paranormal. If you believe there is a ghost attempting to gain your attention, look for natural explanations that could explain the incidents. Be a little skeptical. This approach will help keep you more levelheaded while trying to conclude if incidents are real examples of ghost communication. A rational, open mind is the best tool in determining if the source of a possible haunting is in fact the result of an active ghost. If you are unable to find a normal explanation for the abnormalities you have experienced, it might be time to consider communication with the troubled spirit.

When I investigate an active haunting, I prefer to gather detailed information before attempting to help a ghost that possibly needs my attention. If I can gather enough details from all witnesses, then I might be able to identify who the ghost is and possibly what haunts the mind of the troubled spirit. This improves my chances of helping a disembodied human spirit progress from this world unto the next. It is good to take notes from every witness of the paranormal phenomena, paying particular attention to their impressions and suspicions. Sometimes, witnesses will have a good feeling for the spirit's identity and why the ghost may be lingering with them. Look for details, and if possible, research a location in the hope of learning more about its history and the people who were associated with it.

Recordings made in a haunted location may reveal additional clues about ghosts that can be used to help them. It can be as simple as leaving an audio recorder in an active room and allowing it to record for a bit. Others prefer to ask questions, giving a ghost enough time to answer between queries. Afterward, you simply amplify and analyze the recording, using a computer and headphones to hear if a disembodied person might have responded. These methods for gathering electronic voice phenomena (EVP) can be a great way for a desperate spirit to get a message across to the attentive ear. Utilization of a ghost box, as you have already read, can also be a fantastic way for the skilled user to collect EVP.

Let's suppose you have gathered as much information as possible and are relatively certain that there is a ghost that needs your help. You might even know the person in spirit. What do you do? Allow me to encourage you: You can do this work. You can help a ghost. The first step in helping ghosts is to become open to the idea that we are not separate from those whose bodies have perished. We must cease from believing that people eternally slip away and disappear into nether or celestial worlds, somehow separate from our own. We are eternally in this together. The ghost is another human being, who in essence, is a part of you. Become confident in who you are and your connection with spirit.

You learned that people in spirit are around us, with us. We are not separate from them even if we would like to believe it was so. Only our minds can temporarily divide us from one another. Everyone is a part of us; humanity is an energy comprised of energies. This is important to understand, because everyone will eventually be reunited.

"I have other sheep that are not of this yard: them I must also bring, and they shall hear my voice...and there shall be one flock..." - John 10:16

Working to bring the whole of mankind to an understanding of our oneness is the crux of what helping ghosts is truly about. It is a great and admirable endeavor. Although some disembodied spirits' situations might be difficult to remedy, it is certainly worth the effort. By helping others, honestly, I have found we help to resolve our own issues. We feel better about ourselves when we love one another. By freeing ghosts, by lessening their burdens, we free and enlighten ourselves.

When we choose to help those who have become trapped here after their body expired, we are not only reuniting families in the invisible but also bringing healing and closure to families here on earth. This is especially true for those who are suffering a haunting. People who are troubled by ghosts also receive peace and gain a new understanding of what is taking place around them in spirit.

I want to reiterate that all are worthy of our compassion. Even the most diabolical soul is one who is lost, pained, and in need of love. I understand that we might struggle with the thought of helping the worst type of person. Still, for our own healing we need to forgive, not condemn. We must move beyond our anger and unforgiving disgust toward the unlovable; otherwise, we will be the ones who suffer. When we judge another, we separate a person from us which is not an act of love.

Ah! Pause and think before you seek
To harshly judge another.
You cannot probe the inner life,
You cannot note the soul's dark strife,
Temptations, nor its dangers rife,
Then do not judge another.

- excerpted from *Kindly Judge Another, Good Housekeeping*, Volume 26 – January, 1898

Judgment is a reaction created out of our own fear. Fear causes suffering. Which is better, to heal or condemn? I pose these questions, because some religions have taught us to promote separation and judgment. Helping ghosts is about transcending that old idea, realizing that we can reach into the invisible and help heal those who still suffer. When we judge and label people, we define who they are only within our mind. Our definitions of people are limited. How can we ever adequately describe or begin to understand the depths, experiences, and feelings of another living soul? Furthermore, how can we perfectly define an eternal being by forming a judgment based upon temporary circumstances? It becomes nearly impossible to behold another's goodness when viewing them solely from a biased opinion.

We need to be compassionate toward others, including the lost spirits of human beings. It dawned on me one day that my dog's capacity to love and forgive appears to be far greater than what some of us exhibit toward other people. The life that energizes everyone and everything is loving and forgiving. My dog is simply more in tune with this. We can do the same. Love heals everyone. Love heals ghosts, too. When we express love, we are being patient, understanding, and displaying compassion toward others. Remember to imagine yourself in their predicament. Identify with their suffering in order to understand what they might be feeling. Love people where they are at. What must the hurting person be feeling? What have they suffered? How can we bring love to them and create healing? Although we may not be able to help every ghost, I am comforted by the fact that every lost spirit will have their time to be restored. There will be none lost. One way or another, sooner or later, all spirits will find their way home.

For a ghost to be able to receive love from another, it is necessary to address their fear. It is fear that prevents them from understanding the truth of their state, temporarily blocking out the love that will heal their thinking. Remember, no matter what excuse a spirit may have for remaining earthbound, the reason behind the behavior is always fear. Similar to love, fear is energy, though it can become a very debilitating force. Love dissolves fear. A ghost's energy of fear transforms into love when the spirit becomes free. You can actually feel the energy change as they enter the light of peace. To help ghosts, we must be free from fear ourselves. Not only can fear cause the mind to create what is not there, but it can also cause us to believe things to be more powerful and precarious than what they really are. Fear intensifies situations. Although you may be, at first, afraid to help a discarnate person, understand that this is common and that you can choose to remain strong and not show your fear. When we fear ghosts, we give them power and submit ourselves to their influence. Be strong. Choose not to give in to fearful thoughts. If we show that we are afraid of ghosts who might behave negatively toward us, we essentially affirm their poor behavior. We are revealing to them that we can be pushed around by things that frighten us. By showing that you are fearless, you remain in control of the situation.

The best way to remain fearless is simply to know you are incorruptible, powerful, eternal energy. Look deeper than your body. When a person is in touch with their permanent core, something wonderful happens; their view on life changes, and they become aware of their inner power. Knowing who you are is the best protection from ghosts that exhibit ill will.

"Know thyself." - Socrates

I shared that we can become awakened to the life-source within us through meditation. Meditation differs from prayer in several ways. When we pray, we talk and do not listen. We present requests, hoping that a higher power will hear us. Meditation is not talking. It is listening for the answers that are bubbling forth from the higher power within you. This is how we mentally *connect* to the spirit energy; whereas prayer is often a reaction out of fear from believing we are *disconnected* from God. The wonderful energy we tap into through meditation is the light that dissolves our fears and the fears of others.

Remember that my experiments and experiences revealed

that we are not alone when we help ghosts. Trust in this. There are others with us in spirit who are highly intelligent and have our best interest at heart. Spirits, especially families and friends of the deceased, will assist us in reaching ghosts who need our help. It is common for enlightened spirits to escort ghosts to those who are able to communicate with them. I have come to expect multiple ghosts to be present with us when we conduct spirit circles. If we are going to help one lost soul, we might as well help all we can. Knowledgeable and helpful spirits will also work to reunite the recently departed with grieving family, especially if creating signs or conveying messages will bring some closure to the greatly bereaved. This heals both the ghost and the grieving loved one.

You might wonder why the task of helping ghosts is not the sole responsibility of enlightened spirits. In other words, why would we need to help ghosts? After all, wouldn't spirits be better equipped to help other spirits? The answer to that question is yes and no. The reason we can be of help to ghosts is due to their mentality; ghosts have their mind focused on the physical plane. Lost spirits will often require interaction with those in the corporal world, sometimes being more willing to communicate with people in the flesh than with spirits. Keep in mind that guilt-ridden ghosts frequently fear other spirits. They could fear they might be godly messengers who have come to drag them away to judgment; or may believe a demon is out to get them. You also learned that ghosts suffering condemnation might hide in shame from the spirit of a loved one. Just the opposite can be true in other cases. Ghosts occasionally seem unable to find the spirits of loved ones due to their emotional state. I am certain there are even more reasons that could explain why earthbound spirits prefer to communicate with people in the flesh. No matter the example, this is where we can play an important role. We can help earthbound spirits become free from condemnation, guilt, and fear. We can work to calm their mind. Then, they can be led to the light by us and other spirits.

Enlightened spirits certainly work with ghosts to help guide them to the light. Many times, they are successful without our help; however, it is up to the ghost to trust another spirit's direction. During ghost rescues, we have found that spirits like to communicate with us in order to help us understand how best to help a lost soul. Be confident, knowing that we have an invisible team in spirit who will help us mediate and confirm our progress. The team will likely include ghosts' relatives who are willing to help lead their lost family members to the light. Even ghosts that are not related have been known to counsel other ghosts before heading to the light themselves! My point is that we are never alone in this endeavor.

I want to make you aware that there are optimal times we can take advantage of that may possibly enhance our ability to communicate with ghosts. We need to consider what we can do to encourage ghosts to interact with us. How can I allow the spirit to remain comfortable? What might make it better for the ghost to communicate? There are several things to consider before making contact with wayward spirits.

It is well known by seasoned paranormal investigators that

ghost communication can be heightened during solar storms and peak geomagnetic activity. This would indicate we might want to pay attention to space weather forecasts. It is also believed that ghost activity can be strengthened up to three days before or after a full or new moon. Having become interested in this theory, I examined the results of some of my investigations and experiments, noticing that many of my ghost communication sessions were heightened near full or new moons. If the moon phase theory is true, it might also explain a rather interesting biblical passage about ghosts and spirits appearing during darkness.

"...there was darkness over all the land...and the graves were opened; and many bodies of the saints who had died were raised...they went into the holy city and appeared to many."

- excerpted from Matthew 27:45, 52, 53

The unusual appearance of darkness possibly describes an eclipse. A solar eclipse is when the sun is darkened for a period of time. The effect can only be caused during a new moon, because the moon passes between the earth and the sun. Therefore, a solar eclipse would potentially create a time of increased ghost activity. Could this explain why the ghosts of people were said to be witnessed after the death of Jesus? I'm not certain about what actually happened 2000 years ago, but it does line up nicely with the moon phase theory.

Ghost investigating during night time has become the norm, but many do not understand the reason behind this, including some paranormal investigators. I certainly cannot deny that some ghost hunting groups choose to search for ghosts at night, because it is often an after-work hobby. Still, there is history behind ghosts and night time activity. Based upon European folklore, the witching hour is believed to be the time between midnight and 3:00 AM where witches, ghosts, and demons are thought to be at their peak of activity. Although the witching hour is superstition, it still has some basis on fact. As I expressed previously, darkness provides a cover for ghosts to hide and feel safer. Their actions are less noticeable when shaded. Not every ghost hides in the dark; some would rather choose daylight for comfort. Ghosts who wish to remain camouflaged are likely to prefer more obscure conditions. Consequently, if we want to increase our chances of communicating with earthbound spirits, I suggest that night time and low-level lighting will create a less stressful environment for the majority of ghosts.

When investigating a haunting, I like to do a walk-through of the residence or building in order to assess where the ghost prefers to dwell. I follow my gut feeling. This spot within the location is more likely to be a place of comfort for the lost spirit. Because I will be invading his or her space, I feel it is necessary to go to where the best communication will be possible. There are no rules that a ghost must obey. A spirit may choose to move away from our presence or come right to us no matter where we are at. Just like people, ghosts may be timid or sociable. Take the time to tune into the environment of the haunted location. Follow your intuition, and listen to your hunches. When walking through rooms and hallways, pay attention to what triggers your senses. Oftentimes, the information I have gathered from witnesses prior to an investigation will correlate nicely with where I might sense the ghost's presence. This is not always the case, so be open to moving around and locating where you feel it best to begin your work.

I should mention that it is not always necessary to be present at the location to help lost spirits transition to the light. Although I prefer to be on-site to assess the situation and communicate with the troubled ghost in-person, sometimes this is simply not possible. Kathy Owen, who lives far away from me in California, once shared that she was undergoing a terrible attack from a ghost that was causing her to feel sick all the time. She was also experiencing chest pains. Kathy felt her ex-husband, "Moose," was in her home, attempting to end her life. Before his death, Moose had made a promise to Kathy. No matter where she lived or who she was with, he would always protect her. After Moose died in prison from a heart attack, she recognized his presence with her at home. Kathy reasoned that perhaps Moose became so attached to her that she might have been suffering from his heart condition and sickness. She worried that maybe he wanted to prematurely end her earthly life, so she could join him in the ethereal realm. Being concerned for Kathy, I wanted to help her. There was no way I could make my way to California. I decided to pursue a three-way conference call including my friend, Laura Lyn, on the line. Laura was more experienced in working with spirits over the telephone. She felt strongly that we could be of help to Kathy. As we listened to Kathy share her ordeal, Laura and I discerned that another ghost was the cause of the problems. He was an angry spirit bent on revenge over a past event involving Kathy. As Kathy listened, we reasoned with the ghost for quite some time, eventually convincing him to depart with loved ones into the light. Immediately, Moose, who had also been there to watch over Kathy, came forward and thanked us. He gave me what I can only describe now as a spirited hug!

It should be obvious by now that I feel the best way we can help ghosts is through communication. Sometimes the communication will break down, so we must remain determined and patient. I can recall many times when working with ghosts that my attempts to reach them seemed to be in vain. Patience has never been my strong suit, but it is a requirement to effectively help spirits. When you feel like giving up, wait. Listen intently within your being, paying attention to the thoughts that come to you for direction. This may take time. Inspiration as to how you can help hurting spirits will eventually come if given enough time. Others will make sure of it. If your attempt at helping a ghost seems futile, be creative and not afraid to think beyond the norm. We can try to use things to trigger responses from spirits, such as speaking forth names of the deceased, handling their former possessions, or including their relatives in the spirit circle process. The idea is to get on the same page with one another. You are looking to establish a connection. Finding common ground is the key to the emotional rescue of another. If that person can identify with you in some way, then it is possible they will be able to hear and consider what you have to offer. Having empathy toward another allows for an emotional connection to be made.

Forming a bond brings understanding; truth and love naturally follow. This is the method I use to free ghosts.

You have learned that emotional turmoil is what holds earthbound spirits captive to this realm; therefore, it is important to momentarily stop their emotional roller coaster. I try and do this by gaining the ghost's attention and speaking about their situation. I want them to pause and examine their actions. If I can get lost souls to recognize the fears that motivate them, then they may become much more willing to leave them behind. My goal is to be perceived as a messenger of truth who can enlighten them and lead them home.

"And you shall know the truth and the truth shall make you free." - John 8:32

Our ability to love one another is a demonstration of the truth that resides within us. When we understand that we are the source of this unending love, it can completely set us free from self-imposed condemnation. Instead of following fear, we can choose to express and experience love; every person has this choice. Show ghosts the good already within them. Souls become peaceful when we help them to see the love and light that is already there.

It is important during attempts at ghost communication that we learn to refrain from calling any disembodied, human being a "ghost," "spirit," "demon," or "it." I have made this mistake and now cringe during ghost investigations when I hear others say, "What does it want?" or "Is there a ghost here who would like to speak with me?" If we want to assist the lost spirits of people, we have to remove all obstacles in their mind as well as our own. Consider how you would feel if you were labeled something other than a person deserving of respect. Although I frequently use the word "ghost" for the purposes of this book, simply understand that it is much better to use words such as "someone" or "person" instead of non-human labels when communicating with spirits.

Even though I want people to view ghosts with compassion, sometimes I have found it necessary to put the needs of the frightened family before the needs of the ghost. No matter how well-intentioned a ghost's actions may be, there are times when a ghost may need to be told enough is enough. Some ghosts, not all, will respect orders given by the head of the household. It may be even more effective if the troubling spirit is given options such as leave the family alone or leave the residence altogether. Even though this does nothing to ease an earthbound spirit's mind, sometimes this works quite well to stop a good-natured spirit from unintentionally frightening family members. Being forthright does cause some ghosts to consider that perhaps their behavior is alarming to those on the receiving end of their attempts at communication, especially if the ghost cares for the person. If the ghost respects the home owner's request, future attempts to communicate with the ghost will typically be welcomed.

If you have a haunting, you might consider establishing ground rules for a ghost who is unwilling to leave and is insistent on remaining a resident. I have known people who have been unsuccessful with aiding a dear, old uncle or beloved grandmother to the light. Given little choice, they opted to tell the loved one that he or she was welcome to stay with them for awhile. They also let the ghost know what behaviors were considered acceptable. These people feel blessed to have their unseen loved ones looking after them. Some ghosts will not respond kindly to the idea of setting terms and will welcome the challenge, like a gauntlet being tossed before them. The most effective method to help ghosts resolve past issues and encourage them to leave a location is not by commanding them to go but reasoning with them. Ask them why they have chosen to remain behind, address their concerns, and then direct them to where they really should want to be. At times, we need to be firm but still with compassion toward their crisis.

Having gathered information from witnesses and my own investigation, as well as following my own intuition, I should have enough insight into the haunting to make my communication with the ghost more effective. Ready to help ghosts cross from this plane to the next, I prefer the evening hours, low-light conditions, and few interruptions to conduct a spirit circle. It is fine to have several people in the room with you, especially if they are spiritually awakened and unafraid. If available, it's wonderful to have a psychic-medium present as confirmation and assistance with speaking to lost spirits. Usually, I like to begin by inviting enlightened spirits to be present to help with the communication as well as welcoming other lost spirits who may be ready for guidance too. I feel it is important to not make any judgment concerning ghosts. I want every lost soul to feel welcome.

"Those who are with us in spirit, I appreciate your assistance. All

those who can hear my voice are welcome to be here and take part."

Next, I prefer to make my intentions known. When we enter another person's house, we are guests to those who live there. Introduce yourself, be polite, and explain the reasons behind your visit. I speak openly that I know others are in the room, that I am there to speak with them, maybe even help them:

My name is Louis and I am here to help those who are lost. I only mean well and hope to speak with everyone who is here. Although some may be afraid, I know you are here with me; I mean you no harm.

Explaining to disembodied spirits that their body is gone can be important. Some ghosts do not recall their moment of death. I like to provide confirmation of that for them. Validating that the body has expired, I encourage the ghost that they are alive and well:

I am here to confirm for you that your body has died. Yet, you are still very much alive. You can hear my voice. You are alright and needn't be afraid. The real person is eternal; you are energy, spirit, and cannot die.

Continuing to explain the ghost's condition, I work to remove fear of death and punishment while attempting to ascertain why the soul has remained earthbound. Many believe that as soon as the body dies, they will be in heaven. This is not necessarily true. Our current frame of mind determines whether we are in a state of bliss or a time of suffering. It is important we let ghosts know that they have chosen to temporarily stall their life-journey, having neglected to head into the light. When attempting to bring back the recollection of a ghost's death, we can mention that they might remember seeing light but for some reason did not head toward it. It is also a good idea to actually explain the light in more detail.

You have remained behind on earth, because for some reason, you did not head into the light. The light was present when your body expired, but you did not go for whatever reason. Perhaps, you were confused or had concerns; maybe you were not able to see the light at the time. The light is the doorway to what you may call "Heaven" and certainly not something to fear. It is the place where your family and friends are, a place you want to be. It is your future and a place of happiness, love, and peace. You may continue your life there without worries, pain, or sorrow. It's time to be with loved ones, and I am here to help guide you there now.

I prefer to inform lost spirits that there could be unresolved business we need to address, some concerns that kept them here on earth. Ghosts need to understand they are living in the past. This causes them to miss out on truly enjoying the present. It is important to let them know that their future is bright with so much more to experience than they could ever imagine.

Express to ghosts that their concerns, their worries, their doubts are really fears. It is important for them to understand that fears are false. There is nothing to fear, absolutely nothing. They must let go of the past and its fears to truly be free. I further express to ghosts that they are forgiven for any and all past mistakes:

What has kept you here has been your own fear. Trapped in the past, you have forsaken the present moment, seemingly leaving a hopeless future. It is time to let the past roll off your back, leave it behind and in its place. Let all worries and doubts, all fearful concerns, go. To forget your past mistakes is to forgive yourself. You should forgive everyone who might have wronged you in the past in order for you to know forgiveness. There is nothing as important. You'll not lose contact with loved ones by choosing to move forward in life, yet you'll gain healing for yourself. By heading to the light, you will learn that there is no lack, there is no loss, and all things will work out for the good. The world that lies ahead is much better than the world we leave behind. You will see everything anew and receive understanding from a much better perspective.

Knowing that some ghosts fear punishment in Hell because of religious beliefs, I like to make them aware that there is no Hell that awaits them; they are in hell right now. Let ghosts hear that hell is a prison of fear they created, a state of mind that they can walk out of at any moment. Their punishment is self-inflicted. Choosing to embrace the light and its cleansing power will transform them, immediately removing souls from judgment and self-condemnation:

Remaining behind here and living in the past has been your hell, something that you suffered needlessly. The light is not Hell but your Heaven; for there really is no hell but what we unknowingly create through our own false beliefs. You are forgiven. Now, forgive yourself. It is time for you to step down off of your emotional carousel and stop the cycle of suffering. You can experience a peace that you have never known. The light will make you feel brand new again, and everything will become right as rain.

It is important to let ghosts know that if they are afraid of the light, the light is not the flames of Hell. It is best described to people as Heaven. A heavenly afterlife is surely desired by most people and thought to be good just like the light is always good. Both are known to be where love, peace, and joy reign supreme. When the time is right, I like to make ghosts aware that they'll feel cleansed, find important answers, and reunite with family and friends in the light. I let them know that their loved ones in spirit are already with them, pleading, desiring to be acknowledged.

"You are a good person. You deserve so much more from life. The darkness you may perceive is the result of feeling lost inside. Your life needs direction, and you may not understand who you are or where you are going. This is temporary and something that is corrected by the light. The light is the good in you; it is part of you. It is your inner sense. Just know that you are forgiven for any and every mistake you might have made in life. You are healed and whole, no longer broken or lost. You are loved. Family and friends are with you now. They love you and want you to go with them into the light. If you see family with you, it is now time to join them."

I enjoy telling hurting spirits that they are good. Some people go through life never hearing or knowing how special they are. Humanity is loving and joyful at heart. They may not be aware of the depth of their soul or even know how to express what's there. Ignorance cannot change the fact that true goodness resides within. Everyone needs to know they are worthy and important. This is not only important for those in the physical world but for those in spirit, too. It is time for understanding to replace suffering. The light is not separate, but is the goodness within everyone. You'll remember that what appears outside of us is really the result of the condition within a soul. Darkness, then, is not something we should view as bad. It is only misunderstanding. I feel we may come to learn that our lives actually benefit from contrast, even causing us to acquire knowledge of ourselves. After all, light is always easier to recognize while there is darkness. This is why we should encourage ghosts to contemplate their predicament. Our assistance just might expand their awareness of the eternal light within, so the internal truth becomes their external reality. As people, when we do not feel loved, we wrongly believe that we are lacking love inside. This means we simply need to mentally reconnect with the love that's already in our hearts. It's the same for ghosts, too. They need to reconnect with what they have temporarily forgotten. When we express love to others, it awakens people to the love that's already within them. Let us not be afraid to express our love to help others rise above their inner fears. Love will remove all darkness, illuminating the path that lies ahead.

After communicating the ideas I shared, it is important to let ghosts know that it is now time for them to leave this world behind and embark upon an exciting journey. What lies ahead is something magnificent! You are now ready to encourage them to find the light and head directly into it. It is good for everyone participating in the spirit circle to focus their intention as a group toward manifesting the light. While this is happening, I prefer to help ghosts envision the light through use of their imagination.

"I want you to imagine your eyes are closed and that the sun is beginning to rise directly behind you. As you think about this, the sun's

rays begin to shine on your back and shoulders, the warmth penetrating your skin. You feel the rays of the sun's light, and it feels good and inviting. These light rays are becoming brighter and brighter and shining all over your body now. Each ray of light is causing every worry and concern to melt away like snow on a hot, July day. You feel the light and its embrace, knowing you are loved and at peace. A person, who has also died and whom you have wanted to see more than anyone else, is now standing with you. Hold out your hand and feel their embrace. Knowing that your loved ones are with you, I want you to turn toward the light, open your eyes and keep walking into it. With each step, you feel waves of love, joy, and peace wash over you. You feel clean and good. Keep heading into the light..."

If all concerns have been addressed, the ghost should slip with ease into the celestial world. It's not uncommon to miss something, so there still may be one last hurdle to overcome. By this point in the process, ghosts often want to transition to the light and may even see it. What sometimes bothers them is the idea of leaving loved ones on earth behind. We must encourage the disembodied spirit to go forth. Explain that even though they will enter into the light, they still will be able to return and visit. Keep encouraging until you know that the ghost has made the transition.

"You may come back here and visit if you like. Do not be afraid to move onward. Keep going...may peace be with you."

Despite your best efforts, if you do not feel the person in spirit has left, then remain open to your feelings. What thoughts come to you during the spirit circle? Sometimes, we are quick to discount them. There may be something very simple to address that will cause the ghost to feel free to depart. It is important that we do not give up easily. Press forward, remaining determined. I must emphasize that patience and communication are the keys to helping ghosts. If the ghost has not left, the communication was not good enough at addressing whatever is still bothering the troubled soul. Find the problem and solve it. This is the task of a good ghost investigator.

I choose to reveal the light to ghosts through patiently speaking with them until they are ready to move beyond this world. Compassionate pleas seem to be able to break through ghosts' mental barriers that were, at one time, debilitating. This does not mean that my specific method is the only way ghosts can be helped. I am sure there are many different ways; for example, I am aware of people who are able to welcome a lost spirit's energy into their body and simply love them through to the light. My friend and Director of *SIGHT*, Christopher Reed, explains his ability much better than I can:

When SIGHT forms a spirit circle, I can feel energies all around me as we bring the earthbound ghost to the circle using our energies to help them to the light. Many times, I have had my body used as a host for these ghosts who may be unsure, scared, or just flat-out refuse to leave. With the exception of negative entities who desire to just do harm more than anything else, I usually use myself as a guide and tool to help spirits on their way to the light by allowing them to use my energy. I seem to best channel ghosts that are unsure or who fear the light. I can feel their energy swirling about me and enter me. When that happens, I seem to tense up and get very cold, as many in SIGHT have witnessed and felt. Then it seems I feel paralyzed, and it's like passively watching someone else. I can sense their thoughts, see what they see through my eyes, and feel their emotions. The ghosts have free will to speak through me, too. My energy, along with the group's energy and our communication, helps the earthbound ghost or energy to pass from within me and unto the light. This feels like a large vacuum pulling the very breath from me as the ghost leaves my body. It can be a very emotional time for me, feeling their warmth and peace as they travel on through to the light.

Chris' account of spirit rescue beautifully illustrates that compassionate communication is the best way to help ghosts. No matter the method, love should always be the power behind the practice.

Helping the ghosts of children to the light often depends upon our ability to express love. Children are more attracted to loving, kind people. Although the goal is the same, the method of reaching the mind of a ghost child often needs to be much simpler. Getting the child spirit to trust and listen to your direction is sometimes difficult, especially if we appear frightening, impatient, or unloving. Being kind, harmless, and approachable is the best way to communicate with the ghosts of children. Once their trust is gained, then you can ease their fears and guide them to loved ones. Reuniting the ghosts of children with deceased parents, grandparents, or siblings can quickly complete the process. Don't be afraid to ask for their loved ones to come forth. They are likely already there with the child. Most child ghosts seem to be lost and looking for family or friends. We just help them to connect with each other. Many times, this is all we need to do. I have also heard of people who prefer to lovingly embrace the ghost of a child and usher their spirit to the light in this manner. Whatever method we choose, we become the bridge to help them find their way back home. If we prefer to talk them through, then we can describe the light more simply, such as being a happy and fun place. This can ease their transition. Remember, keep it simple. If after your best efforts the child ghost still has not left, then there is still fear blocking the way that must be addressed.

How can we tell if a ghost has finally made the transition from this world to the next? You will know it by the change in atmosphere. Fear, anger, and suffering produce negative energy that is draining and discernable. Have you ever walked into a room where somebody just argued, and you felt you could cut the tension with a knife? Negativity from ghosts can also be perceived by those skilled in ghost investigation. It is even possible for an irritated spirit to express anger that can be tangibly felt as heat on the skin by those in the same room. Often, it is a heated desire to combat or argue with people who have caused the spirit's temper to flare. Ghosts can indeed be felt. When ghosts transcend the earthly realm and move on in their life-journey, the energy shifts to one of tranquility. This feeling of peace is never draining. It is joyous and extremely loving. Often, ghosts who have reunited with family will express their thanks through expressions of love and gratitude toward those who aided them. When we help ghosts, the end of the process is "the release." Look for the energy of love, peace, and joy to be released when the task of helping a ghost is accomplished. It may be felt as goose bumps by those who are fortunate enough to witness such a transformation. This love can also be felt as waves within a person, like flowing water of liquid love.

"...out of his body shall flow rivers of living water. (...this he spoke about the spirit...)"

- John 7:38-39

The release of love we share by helping ghosts always deeply awakens me to the energy that connects us all. Once a ghost has moved on, I suppose there is nothing left to do except reflect upon the experience, remaining ever grateful for the opportunity that was afforded us. We can take great comfort in knowing that helping lost spirits is a part of reuniting all of humanity, essentially bringing healing to ourselves.

In Summation

The following steps summarize how I prefer to help ghosts. Always remember that we heal lost spirits by communicating with them, not by ignoring them. Some ghosts will be easier to help than others, so remain patient and do not give up. Free the mind and you will free the ghost. Always affirm the good, showing compassion and remaining empathetic. The goal is to undo ghosts' fear and offer love in return.

1. Make no judgment, choosing to help all lost spirits.
2. Declare your intentions and acknowledge ghosts by addressing them.
3. Explain that their body has died, but that they are still alive in spirit.
4. Explain that they have not moved on in life, having neglected to go to the light.
5. Make ghosts aware that by remaining behind they are living in the past, which is fearful.
6. Let ghosts know that their fear is false. They have nothing to fear.
7. Affirm that the ghost is good, worthy of something better. They are forgiven.
8. Explain to the ghost that there is no Hell, for they have created their own hell.
9. Tell ghosts that no further condemnation or punishment awaits them.
10. Work to help the ghost resolve any unfinished business.

11. Explain that the light is good; it is peace, joy and love, what they may call "heaven."
12. Make ghosts aware that their loved ones are in the light and with them now.
13. Let ghosts know it is time they move onward in their life-journey by entering the light.
14. Tell ghosts that they may return and visit loved ones here on earth.
15. Encourage all lost spirits to re-establish ties with their loved ones in the light. This is powerful.

The following are some tips I have put together for those who wish to work with the ghost box in order to communicate with ghosts and spirits. If you fear ghosts, you should not attempt to communicate with them until you have overcome your concerns. The ghost box can be a wonderful way to gather more information about a haunting. To make ghost box recordings, you will need to either make or purchase a hacked radio that sweeps the AM or FM bands. (For more information, visit angelsghosts.com/ghost_box.)

1. In order for the ghost box to work properly, there must be AM or FM broadcast signals. Otherwise, you'll only be working to record EVP with white noise, which will also work but not nearly as well. I have achieved good results with both the AM and FM bands. If your area has few radio stations, the ghost box might not work well unless you are able to strengthen the antenna. Electronic stores, such as *Radio Shack*, sell antenna boosters that may work nicely for you.

2. When using the ghost box, it is good to take notes and record every session. Some messages will be heard live, while others will be discovered later while listening to the audio with a pair of headphones. A pair of decent headphones is a must.

3. Use a simple, hand-held audio recorder that can be purchased at most electronics stores. Placing it near the ghost box speaker works best to record the sessions. The ghost box volume should not be too loud, or your recording will be ruined. You want to be able to hear your own voice asking questions over the sweeping radio noise. Allow enough time between questions for answers. I prefer recording short sessions of only a few minutes, as it makes it easier to analyze than having one long recording to work your way through.

4. Upload your ghost box recordings onto a computer by using a USB cable and software that should have come with your audio recorder. Once you have the audio files on your computer, it is necessary to analyze them. If you do not have audio editing software, you can download a version for free, such as Audacity or Wavepad. You do not need complex, expensive software to analyze your ghost box recordings.

5. Open your audio file with the audio editing software and listen to it closely with your headphones. Work through each file slowly, listening for answers to your questions that are credible. The longer the answer the better. Phrased answers that are relevant to your

questions are preferred. If the volume of the recording is too low, then amplify it to hear the audio better.

6. When you find a section of audio you would like to save, simply cut it out of the original file. To clean it up, I recommend trimming out irrelevant audio fragment noise when possible, leaving the spirit's response (preferably the question with answer). If the message is fast, you may consider slightly slowing the segment down and amplifying it before cutting it out of the original audio file. Trim away useless audio fragments.

7. Practice, practice, practice. The more you work with the ghost box, the better your recordings will become. Your ear will also become better attuned to hearing the messages found within the audio. As the radio sweeps either the AM or FM band, it is jumping from frequency to frequency. This sometimes causes a rhythm within the recording that you will learn to tune out. Also, you will notice that once you begin communicating regularly with ghosts and spirits, the communication will become easier. Sometimes, you may experience multiple spirits attempting to communicate at once, talking over each other in excitement!

Electronic Voice Phenomena can also provide more details that will enable you to help ghosts. The following are some tips to recording ghost voices called EVP. There are many techniques to recording EVP, but as always, the more you work with it, the better your results will be.

1. Use a simple, hand-held, audio recorder to record

EVP. You may elect to make recordings at the same time and place each day to set a schedule of sort with spirits. Some people prefer only to record while in haunted locations in order to focus on communication from ghosts.

2. Ask questions, but be sure to allow enough time for answers. EVP messages are typically short phrases. It's always good to keep detailed notes of all your EVP sessions.

3. When recording EVP during ghost investigations, it is sometimes better to carry on conversations with others in the room while the recorder is on. Many times, voices of ghosts are recorded while people are talking. It's as if they prefer to interact with us. I also suspect that human voices help carry disembodied spirit voices, making them more likely to be recorded.

4. Do not whisper or make soft vocalizations, such as groans, grunts, or any expressions, when doing EVP work. Try and tag any odd noises or confusing sounds that occur during the EVP session. Identify it aloud during the recording right after the sound or noise occurs. This will help to eliminate false evidence.

5. Audio files should be uploaded to a computer and analyzed using audio editing software, such as Audacity, with a decent pair of headphones. With EVP, it is necessary to amplify the sound files quite a bit for analysis. Most EVPs are very subtle, low-volume whispers, so you have to listen closely. Cut out any

segments of EVP from within the original audio file and save. For more information on recording and analyzing EVP, I suggest visiting the *American Association of EVP* website, AAEVP.com.

You can learn to hear messages from your higher consciousness. The following is a simple meditation technique I have used for years. With some practice, you should be able to relax your body and mind, enabling you to connect with your deepest being. Listening to our heart is where we gain higher understanding, as well as the ability to tune-in to spirit communication:

1. Lying or sitting down in a comfortable position, close your eyes and begin by relaxing your toes. After your toes are relaxed, then relax your calf muscles, thighs, and pelvis.
2. Continue to relax your body. Let the muscles in your fingers, stomach, arms, neck, and head become completely relaxed. Your entire body should now be completely in a relaxed state.
3. Now, you need to relax your mind. Let go of all fears, all concerns, and all thoughts. Be at peace. With practice, I am able to quiet my mind quite quickly by allowing every care or concern to just drift away, seeking to be in the present moment. If you struggle with relaxing your mind, simply focus on hearing your heart beat. Listen intently for the beat of your heart. Whether or not you hear it does not matter. The mind is now focused on one thing and not dwelling on anything else

but listening. Relax for a while as you listen.

4. Remaining in this relaxed state, you may think thoughts of gratitude. Being thankful can open us up to our deepest being. When I enter in, I feel intense love, joy, and peace. This is a cleansing place, a state of bliss and relaxation. When I reach this point, I am at one with everything, and I feel deeply loved. I enjoy soaking in this feeling for awhile. Enjoy the moment. You, too, will feel refreshed and whole when this occurs.

5. Now, listen intently. What do you hear from within you? This is the voice that comes to us as knowing, for it is our higher consciousness that guides us. As we become familiar with this voice and state, we will depend upon it for direction in our lives. This is the voice I follow to help troubled spirits.

6. You may also wish to focus on a person whom you wish to contact. Mentally ask them questions. What answers to the questions do you hear within you?

7. Be patient with yourself and allow time for responses or answers to your questions. The more you practice meditation, the better your discernment.

I must mention that if you struggle with religious ideas and fears that may interfere with helping ghosts, I suggest you read my first book entitled, *Jesus Religion: A Critical Examination Of Christian Insanity.* Having been a former church elder, I share historical, biblical, and logical insights that undo frightening beliefs concerning demons, hell, sin, punishment, and more.

You can learn more at JesusReligion.com.

For additional information about *Helping Ghosts*, please visit HelpingGhosts.com.

For more information concerning ghosts and spirits, be sure and visit my website *Angels & Ghosts* at AngelsGhosts.com.

Index

Resources

Recommended Reading

1) *Ghosts: True Encounters with the World Beyond*, Hans Holzer, Black Dog & Leventhal Publishers

2) *The Unquiet Dead*, Dr. Edith Fiore, Ballantine Books

On-Line Resources

1) *Angels & Ghosts*, Louis Charles, http://AngelsGhosts.com

2) *Jesus Religion*, Louis Charles, http://JesusReligion.com

3) *Angel Reader Laura Lyn*, http://AngelReader.net

4) *American Association of Electronic Voice Phenomena*, http://www.AAEVP.com

5) *Frank's Box*, Frank Sumption, http://PurpleAlienGirl.Tripod.com/

6) *EVP and ITC Discussion Group*, http://Tech.Groups.Yahoo.com/group/EVP-ITC/

7) *Keyport Paranormal*, Steve Hultay, http://KeyportParanormal.com

8) NOAH *National Weather Service Space Weather*, http://SWPC.NOAA.gov

9) *Audacity Audio Editor*, http://Audacity.SourceForge.net

10) *Lake Isabella Paranormal Society*, Kathy Owen, http://TheLIPS.Ning.com

11) *Mountaineer Paranormal*, Polly Gear, http://MountaineerParanormal.Ning.com

---

It has been a pleasure to work with Louis Charles. His enthusiasm with helping ghosts is obvious when working with him. Louis has a special gift, understanding how to help souls who have become lost and confused. His NO FEAR approach is refreshing and contagious. Louis gets it; love is the only way to help earthbounds "see the light" through educating them and releasing the shackle of fear that has prevented them from moving on to their eternal truth.

Louis and I have worked together on dozens of case studies. We have seen and heard tragic and sad stories from earthbound spirits. Putting the puzzle together is always fascinating. When a person moves on to their enlightened destiny, it is extremely exhilarating.

Please take the words from this book and move forward to help the lost ones who dearly need to transition. You will find yourself in a whole new place when bringing attention to these people who are forgotten. Their banging, clamoring, and footfalls are a cry out saying, "We exist!" Listen to what they have to say, and offer them a hand.

Blessings,
Laura Lyn
Psychic Medium and Author of "Healing with the Angel Rays"